Neurospeak

Neurospeak

Transforms Your Body, While You Read

Robert Masters

QUEST BOOKS
The Theosophical Publishing House

Wheaton, Ill. U.S.A.
Madras, India/London, England

The Theosophical Publishing House
P.O. Box 270
Wheaton, IL 60189-0270

A publication of the Theosophical Publishing House,
a department of the Theosophical Society in America.

*This publication made possible with
the assistance of the Kern Foundation.*

Library of Congress Cataloging-in-Publication Data

Masters, Robert E. L.
    Neurospeak / by Robert Masters.
        p.   cm.
    ISBN 0-8356-0707-0 : $12.00
    1. Mind and body.   2. Consciousness.   I. Title.
BF161.M375   1994
299´.934—dc20   94-28357
                                                      CIP

        9 8 7 6 5 4 3 2   *   95 96 97 98 99

This edition is printed on acid-free paper that meets the
American National Standards Institute Z39.48 Standard

I dedicate this book to the memory of my grandfather, William Leslie Leeper.

As I experienced him, he was the least flawed and most unconditionally loving human being I have known. Because of him I have been able to be faithful to my essence.

CONTENTS

ACKNOWLEDGMENTS

NEUROSPEAK emerges at a confluence of psychophysical re-education and some other kinds of communication speaking to deeper levels of the person than are reached by language as ordinarily used. Psychophysical re-education and such subcortical linguistics are natural allies and belong together as each expands and enriches the other. I would like to acknowledge as helping to create this alliance the following pioneers, each of whom made his own outstanding and original contributions, and each of whom also provided me with some human interactions which were important and enriching:

Wilfred Barlow

Milton H. Erickson

Moshe Feldenkrais

Thomas Hanna

Because of the work of these men, we have not only a new vision of human possibilities, but also some new and potent ways of making them accessible.

FOREWORD

by Marilyn Ferguson

In *The Autobiography of a Yogi*, Paramahansa Yogananda, the founder of Self-Realization Fellowship, recounted a story about his teacher Sri Yukteswar.

At one point in his youth Yukteswar became seriously ill and lost considerable weight. During his convalescence he visited his guru, Lahiri Mahasaya, and while there explained the cause of his poor health.

On hearing the explanation Lahiri Mahasaya said, "So, you made yourself sick and now you think you are thin. But I am sure you will feel better tomorrow."

The next day Yukteswar thanked his teacher exultantly, "Sir, with your blessings, I feel much better today."

Lahiri Mahasaya said, "Your condition was indeed quite serious, and you are still frail. Who knows how you might feel tomorrow?"

Indeed the next day Yukteswar was again weak, and Lahiri Mahasaya said, "So, once more you indispose yourself."

Over a period of days Yukteswar's ups and downs corresponded precisely to Lahiri Mahasaya's statements, and finally he realized the lesson his guru had been trying to teach him.

"What is this?" Lahiri Mahasaya said. "One day you say to me, 'I am well,' and the next day you say, 'I am sick.' It isn't that I have been healing or indisposing you. It is your own thoughts that have made you alternately weak and strong."

Yukteswar asked, "If I think I am well and that I have regained my former weight, will it be so?" Lahiri Mahasaya responded, "It is so." At that moment Yukteswar felt his strength and weight return.

Yogananda summarized the lesson: *"Thought is the matrix of all creation. . . ."* Many philosophers and teachers throughout history have made this point. The power of thought to create physical effects is at the heart of many spiritual teachings. It is the basis for hypnosis and a host of therapies. "As a man thinketh, so he is." "Thoughts are things."

Scientific research bears this out. Our brains and bodies are affected not only by light and darkness, temperature and humidity, time of day, and sugar highs, but also by cultural beliefs, holiday blues, prayer, and expectations. Our cognitions are biochemical events with biochemical consequences. Some of the findings are remarkable. Elderly men who took part in a Harvard study showed the reversal of certain indices of aging after a three-day immersion experience in which they imagined themselves to be twenty years younger.

Our brains respond to images quite literally. Imagined events have a physical effect. If you imagine hard physical exertion, your heart will begin to race. Experiments have shown that our inner vision is subject to the same optical illusions as our outer. Emotions and attitudes can predispose an individual to particular illnesses. It is well known that certain emotional profiles are likelier than others to lead to cancer or heart disease. And whereas cancer patients are often unusually pliable people, women with cervical cancer tend to score higher on measures of hostility. And among men, hostility and not hard work turns out to be the culprit in the connection between "Type A" behavior and heart disease.

Inspired by Michael Murphy's compendium of bodily transformations, *The Future of the Body,* participants in two year-long experimental programs at Esalen

(1992, 1993) were able to envision, affirm, and achieve measurable goals of physical change—an increase in height, for example.

NEUROSPEAK democratizes the process. With this highly original book in hand, we can literally sense that we have been missing a lot of the action. We become aware of that mysterious human be-ing Clyde Ford calls "the Sage in the Temple." Robert Masters has discovered a way to speak to the mind of the body simply and elegantly so that the reader might experience the vast intelligence that moves us. He teaches us a respectful tone, a way to approach the Sage. This is important, because we already have an instinctual knowledge that we can command the body in a crisis ("You can't get sick now!"), but we have not known how to engage it in dialogue.

NEUROSPEAK is like an invitation to the dance. Few experiences are more uncanny than the personal discovery that the body somehow responds exquisitely to words, printed as well as spoken. Through the medium of language, kinesthetic images are evoked. Muscles respond subtly but surely as they are described. Suggestion leads to image which triggers spontaneous response.

NEUROSPEAK had its genesis in a rich body of prior work. It is the product of the author's long fascination with human potential and a specific interest in how our bodies respond to imagined scenes in literature. During the years he has been developing and refining his therapeutic methods, Bob Masters found the time to write or co-author twenty-five books, among them *The Goddess Sekhmet and the Way of the Five Bodies*, *The Varieties of Psychedelic Experience*, *Mind Games*, and *Listening to the Body* (with his wife, Jean Houston).

This passion for work was aided in his earliest years by a remarkable grandfather, a letter carrier and a great lover of learning. Masters learned to read at three, and at four he was reciting to adult Bible classes. His grandfather regaled him with Norse, Greek, and Roman legends; part Indian, he passed along to Bob Indian lore and taught him how to track and hunt with bow and arrow. He talked to him about rocks, trees, and nature spirits. "And then my interest in mythology expanded to include Edgar Allan Poe and science fiction and shamanism," he recalls.

Bob joined the Navy at seventeen, an act of rebellion toward his father, who wanted him to go to West Point. After the Second World War ended, he worked in Germany during the occupation. He studied at the University of Marburg and then lived in Paris for a year. He also studied at the Alexander Institute in London.

Around 1947 Masters became intrigued by the ideas of Wilhelm Reich, who had broken with Sigmund Freud because he had come to believe that orthodox analysts were limiting themselves. Since neuroses could manifest in the body, Reich wanted to learn more about how the body dealt with trauma. Reich believed that psychological health could be achieved by reorganizing the body.

In 1954 Masters found that the body's response to suggestion is dramatically accelerated by psychedelics, and he began a systematic study of peyote on a weekly basis, with himself as subject. "I'd studied informally with Jean-Paul Sartre," he recalls now, "and existentialism had inflicted a lot of ideas I wanted to be rid of. I found the psychedelics enabled me to maintain a focus of concentration."

He had been preparing himself to become a professor of philosophy. Now the fascination with literature reasserted itself, and he wanted to be a poet or a novelist instead. He went to Texarkana, Texas, where he edited a newspaper and wrote some poetry. He later worked at the *Houston Post*.

Meeting Milton Erickson rekindled his early interest in hypnosis. However, he was more interested in the possibility of heightening sensation than he was in therapy. He had already discovered through psychedelics that in an altered state the body can respond in seconds. The fact that voluntary responses could be influenced gave him the idea that involuntary responses might also have open channels. And here was Erickson, doing just that, creating experimental blindness and deafness in his hypnosis subjects.

It was well-known that the hypnotic suggestion of a burn can produce a blister. In this kind of "virtual reality," as Masters calls it, the brain is unable to distinguish between the images and the objective reality. He found, for example, that if an individual had become paralyzed at fourteen years old, the paralysis sometimes disappeared when he was regressed to age thirteen, unless the paralysis was caused by a damaged spine.

During this period Masters heard a story that impressed him deeply. In one of the Scandinavian countries a man had been accidentally locked in the freezer compartment of a train. He was found dead, with every clinical symptom of having frozen, but the freezer hadn't been turned on. His imagery of cold was fatal. This story dramatized the clinical potential of imagery, and it became easier to accept other imagery-induced phenomena, like the disappearance of tumors. The brain can be deceived. And whatever the brain can organize, Masters says now, the body will execute.

That's the simple secret of NEUROSPEAK. Movements are described in such a way that the mind must create images, *whether or not it is a conscious process.* These images trigger effects in the motor cortex, where muscular activity is initiated. Then there is an involuntary response to the images in the muscular skeletal system, and the brain is obliged to move, say, the ankle.

Masters has found that if someone is paralyzed on one side, a suggestion to the non-paralyzed side can produce a memory of kinesthetic sensation. As that remembered sensation is re-experienced, it moves across the hemispheres so that the other side will move—a little at first, then gradually more.

Masters still emphasizes heightening sensation. After NEUROSPEAK exercises, "the body feels taller and lighter," and "as the emotional tone changes, pleasure increases."

Masters has also developed a series of exercises to reverse aging. Anyone can do the exercises, he says; they don't require a vivid imagination. "It's a matter of maintaining concentration and not letting your mind wander. If you learn to frame the statement, if you use the right images, you can work on heart, blood flow, lymph. The movement will happen."

The NEUROSPEAK phenomena speak volumes about our creative potential as well as about body function. The world that seemed so solid becomes more fluid, and that is kind of an endorsement for general creativity. It asks us, "How real is real?" The truism that "thoughts are things" takes on new meaning.

NEUROSPEAK is appropriate for an increasingly mythic time when the boundaries between the material and immaterial worlds have become blurred, and anything seems possible. Scientific and popular literature on the near-death experience is rapidly changing our image of death. We seem to be somewhat interdimensional creatures, designed to play the edges. The war between materialists, who try to nail everything to a neuron, and mentalists, who want to walk on water, becomes irrelevant.

NEUROSPEAK walks the fine line of dialogue, and it raises questions: Who or what is this being that is reading or hearing? If the body listens so attentively, what else does it hear? What about those disparaging comments we make about ourselves, the worries we voice, or the gratuitous violence we beam in via television? Are we responsible for our imaginations?

The words of Robert Masters echo: *Whatever the brain can organize, the body will execute.* A warning, a promise. If we want to turn ourselves and our societies around, this is the conversation we need to have. The movement will happen, he said. Let the movement begin in these pages.

1

WHAT IS NEUROSPEAK?

It is rare that we ever have truly unique experiences. This little book, however, will surely provide its readers with experiences which *are* unique. The uniqueness may or may not be in the end the result of any particular chapter, or of the book as a whole, but lies rather in the fact that significant bodily changes will be occurring in response to almost every paragraph, in some cases, to every sentence.

At the conclusion of a chapter or "exercise," the reader may discover such changes as the following: that one foot or hand moves better than the other and is also more clearly sensed; that the body has somehow become a bit looser or taller or more erect; that altered states of consciousness have been experienced, leading to altered visual and other perceptions of the environment; and that a variety of changes of different kinds have been experienced from one exercise to the next.

The reader may or may not have experienced such bodily changes and altered states of consciousness in the past. However that may be, it is extremely unlikely that such experiences have ever been repeatedly, and in detailed and predictable ways, produced *just by reading a book*. I am not speaking just of something like the emotional responses which can very often occur when reading any well-written novel. Rather, I am speaking of a complex process by means of which words are introduced into the central nervous system of the reader in such a manner that very specific and predictable changes occur in the musculoskeletal system, such as the lengthening of particular muscles in order that certain skeletal joints may move more freely. In the case of this book's induction and utilization of altered states of consciousness, what will be experienced by the reader resembles any familiar response to literary stimuli much less than it resembles experiences occurring in trance states. The literary response, for example, is not likely to facilitate self-regulation of brain waves, and neither will it serve to integrate various senses in order to provide an opening towards a cleansing of the doors of perception.

In order to achieve its effects, NEUROSPEAK cannot be read as other books are read, with the intention—conscious or not—of absorbing its contents mentally. Most books are to be thought of as food for the mind; a few books, as food for the spirit. What NEUROSPEAK offers, however, is food for the body. In order that the body should have access to this food as completely as possible, the mind should not—as is its habit—devour the food, but rather should have the intention that what is read will simply *pass through* the mind on its way to the body. The mind's passivity, for instance, will mean that there is no effort at all made by the mind either to understand intellectually or to remember what it is reading.

What the mind must do is focus intently on what is being read, but solely with the intention of being a kind of screen for the body upon which the message—the text of the book—is projected. The mind must not wander, but must be fully committed to being such a screen. Just as a screen does not retain the words or images projected upon it, so there is no reason for the mind to retain anything of what has been read. That message is just for the body, and its most immediate recipient is, of course, the brain and, in quick succession, the spinal cord, the neural pathways to the muscles, then the muscles themselves, so that they may act upon the skeleton according to the message. Some further instructions about how to read the NEUROSPEAK text are provided in Chapter 3.

When the text is read with mind and consciousness well focused, when the concentration is sufficiently complete, certain phenomena will occur to assist the communication process just described. These phenomena will be very largely unconscious—occurring just below the threshold of consciousness—although they may sometimes penetrate the thin barrier which preserves their unconscious occurrence, so breaking through, in minor but at least recognizable ways, into consciousness. The reason why these phenomena—mostly micromovements of the muscles—are unconscious is simply that they are so small. It is not that one is intending, as with some hypnotic procedures, to generate effects either in or from the unconscious mind.

On the other hand, it has already been stated emphatically that the conscious mind is to participate in the NEUROSPEAK process as minimally as possible. Certainly, what is described in the text is *not* to be executed voluntarily by the conscious mind. The text may state, for example, that one shoulder can move up, or forward, or down, or back, thus making circles by means of rotations of the shoulder joint. This account of possible shoulder movements is absolutely not intended as an instruction to the person to make those movements consciously and voluntarily. Quite the contrary, the mind is to be as passive as possible, doing *nothing* voluntarily, and refraining from initiating bodily activities. Only when the mind is thus passive does the central nervous system have the best opportunity to make its own comparatively pure responses to the text.

What happens, then, when the mind of the reader allows those words describing shoulder movements or other movements to *pass through* it? In response to those words, the brain involuntarily creates an image illustrative of whatever actions the words may be describing. Then, almost as quickly as it creates images, the brain sends out messages to appropriate muscles which, in turn, make minute movements—micromovements—of kinds which, if those movements were larger, would result in the consciously sensed and observable movements described in the text, at which the micromovements barely hint.

Those micromovements will only get into consciousness if they become, so to speak, excessive—casting off, or breaking through the restraints which ordinarily govern them. Then, the person becomes aware of small but distinct involuntary movements and also probably of the need to inhibit those movements consciously if they are not to become still larger.

Most readers will have experiences of this at one point or another in the text, having those particular experiences for any number of reasons which may be quite individual and idiosyncratic. The experience will likely be one of trying to restrain a fairly strong impulse or tendency to carry out objectively movements just read about. The reader may even discover, all at once, that she or he is in the process of doing those movements and doing them in a way that can even approximate the full range of the movements as they are set forth in the text.

With rare exceptions, no particular *described* movement is of any great significance in bringing about the changes intended to occur by the end of the exercise. Rather, the effects occur predictably as the consequence of quite a number of different described movements, carefully arranged as to sequence, and which together have a cumulative effect which produces the intended outcome—greater shoulder mobility, greater hand sensitivity, better posture, different sense of self and the world, or whatever the intended outcome was for a particular exercise.

The "bodygames" you will "play" in this book range from the fairly simple to the quite complicated. They say a good deal about the body's capacities for responding to language, even when the suggestibility of the body has not been enhanced either by means of emotional components or by the induction of states of consciousness which lie beyond the individual norm and the cultural reality consensus.

There are states of consciousness and emotional contexts which increase enormously the body's ability—and tendency—to change in response to both images and verbal expressions. One can well imagine how a novelist who understands this process sufficiently could bring about a wide variety of bodily states—interacting with emotional states and depth levels of consciousness—to create experiences of kinds which literature has not heretofore achieved. Writers have certainly attempted this, but NEUROSPEAK opens up a way of bringing about a wider range of responses, possibly even including ones of such profundity as religious and mystical experiences (by, for example, inducing a state of de-differentiation, loss of ego boundaries, and a consequent experience of oneness with some larger reality).

Since NEUROSPEAK can demonstrably be used—as it is in this book—to bring about quite significant changes in the central nervous system, the muscles, and the skeleton, it seems likely that it can also be used to effect changes in body organs and may perhaps be able to reach *any and all* body parts and processes. Since it does not put its faith in some hypothesized unconscious knowledge or wisdom—as is the case with many hypnotic procedures—it may have even more specific, predictable, and far-reaching medical and other therapeutic applications. Research will have to explore the possibilities for science, just as writers will have to explore the possibilities for literature.

The foregoing should provide the reader with a preliminary understanding of what underlies the method called NEUROSPEAK. After the exercises have been experienced, some further explanation is provided in the Afterword to elaborate upon what has been said here.

2

WHAT WILL I ACHIEVE?

The results of doing NEUROSPEAK exercises will vary quite a lot from one individual to the next. Among other things, the outcome will depend on whether the exercises in the book coincide with the problems and needs of a particular reader. The outcome will also be dependent on the quality and focus of consciousness brought to the reading of the exercises. If some exercises are effective while others are not, either of the factors mentioned above may provide the explanation.

NEUROSPEAK—this book—affords the possibility of making important specific changes in the organization and functioning of various parts of a human body. More important, this little book is a way of gaining exciting new knowledge about a means by which the human body can be changed. I think of the book as providing entertainment as well as self-knowledge, offering readers experiences such as they have never had access to before.

To get back to likely outcomes, however, the vast majority of readers should come away from this book with an expanded, improved, and more accurate body image. That is to say, you should sense more of your body and you should sense it more clearly, as well as more accurately. That opens the way to a healthier and more efficient use of your body and brings mind and body into closer coincidence—both very much to be desired.

You are going to read about many kinds of movements, some of which you would never ordinarily do, or even think about doing. Then those movements—which in fact were done by you at some earlier period of your life—will be reintroduced into your movement repertoire. This will happen because of the micromovements, microsensings, and sensory images which occur as a result of your reading. Those, in turn, will free up previously inhibited patterns of cells in the motor cortex of your brain. Then, to the extent that such disinhibition actually does occur, a "spillover effect" will also bring about some disinhibition in adjacent areas of your brain, in all probability freeing up previously blocked abilities to think and to feel.

NEUROSPEAK will also probably—again, and always, for the truly conscious and concentrated reader—change and expand somewhat your self-image, your awareness of yourself as a totality. You may have a stronger belief in your body's malleability or susceptibility to self-directed or other-directed change for the better. You will understand and know, at fundamental levels of your being, that almost nothing about you is truly fixed. *When you know this, and really believe it, then the way is much more open for you to change in any way at all.* This includes the physical, mental, emotional, and also the spiritual dimensions of your being. It will further embrace such components and attributes as intelligence, imagination and will, balance, creativity, morality, and more. The message of NEUROSPEAK is that just as words, ideas and images can forge mental and bodily shackles around us, so then knowledgeable use of them can set us free—and free at any level of our being.

When we speak of "exercise" in the sense of NEUROSPEAK, it should be understood that we are speaking of approaches which aim at changes of the kinds just mentioned. Naturally, the human organism also requires for its health and for its harmony, good nutrition and intelligent application of those kinds of familiar physical exercises aimed at producing cardiovascular fitness, strength, and other kinds of fitness, including maintenance of the body at a desirable weight. Those are the more superficial levels of exercise, but their importance cannot be overestimated. The more far-reaching changes that embrace the unified interactions of the body/mind system will always be more effectively achieved when the body is well fed, well functioning in all its internal organs, and strong of bone and muscle.

But think, too, of NEUROSPEAK as a kind of bodygame. Allow yourself experiences of it as a novel way of pleasure and enjoyment, a fun-oriented approach to unfolding self-knowledge.

Finally, there is much material here to awaken and seize the imagination of both the scientist and the literary artist. There remain to be discussed and developed NEUROSPEAK applications in neurology, rehabilitation therapies, gerontology, psychotherapy and other areas of psychology, psychiatry and consciousness research, as well as in the writing of fiction and perhaps poetry. The author eagerly and with much curiosity awaits those kinds of developments and applications.

3

How To Do the Exercises

How you do the NEUROSPEAK exercises will determine the results you get from them. This fact will be restated repeatedly, in one way or another, throughout the book. Experience has shown that such reminders are necessary. That is because you are being asked to read in a way that is different from the habitual reading pattern which has been established for many years—with some of you, for many decades.

You are asked to do your reading in a setting that is as conducive as possible to undistracted reading. That might mean, among other things, a room where the telephone will not ring, where other people will not come and go, and where sounds from the external world are as minimal as it is possible for you to arrange.

Other than that, you do not need very much apart from yourself and your copy of NEUROSPEAK. You should wear loose and comfortable clothing and, unless it would be distracting, you should have your feet bare. You should have a table or desk or some other surface on which to rest your book. And you should have a chair that is comfortable but with a bottom firm enough so that you do not sink down into it. Your chair could have arms or not, as you prefer. If possible, try a chair with arms and a chair without arms to discover which kind works best for you.

In addition to having an objective space that is free from distractions, you should also have a subjective space that is as free as possible from distractions. Do not read this book when you are too preoccupied with other matters to give your complete attention to what you are reading. Try to give yourself plenty of time, so that you will never rush your experience because you have to get on to something else. Do not undertake to do any reading just because you feel you ought to do it.

Reading and "doing" the bodygame that is NEUROSPEAK should be something that you want to do, not something that you feel that you must do or need to do. It is a matter of well established fact that human beings learn much better when they are doing what they want to do rather than what they feel compelled to do, no matter whether that compulsion is interior or exterior. People learn best of all when learning is pleasurable—and doing the NEUROSPEAK learning can be pleasurable as well as exciting. What you are doing is novel for you, and you do not know what the outcome will be. The exercises are brief, potentially quite beneficial, and whatever the end of a particular chapter of the book will be for you, it will certainly be a surprise.

As you read, be sure that you are mindful enough to continue to sit comfortably. You should shift your position as little as possible. It is especially important that you do not cross your legs and feet, or arms and hands. In the context of doing a NEUROSPEAK exercise, doing so will confuse your nervous system and prevent your making the responses you should make.

Most human nervous systems are rational and healthy enough to be hedonistic—seeking pleasure and avoiding pain. It is rare that it is justifiable to oppose those tendencies of the healthy nervous system. The NEUROSPEAK exercises will almost certainly give you pleasure if you approach them intending that they will give you pleasure. As you read about many of the movements, you will recognize that they could be done in ways that are sensuous and productive especially of tactile and kinesthetic pleasure—pleasures of touch and pleasures of movement.

You will be reminded repeatedly that it is your focus of consciousness and quality of consciousness that will determine how much you get from NEUROSPEAK. Consciousness will only have a chance to be focused if you provide the kind of objective and subjective circumstances already mentioned. "Focus of consciousness" means the level of concentration which you bring to bear upon your reading. "Quality of consciousness" includes a self-awareness that keeps the concentration from becoming a kind of straining by the will. It is mindfulness which savors your reading, allowing the meanings to flow through the mind with the understanding that they are messages not for the mind but for the body. It is also "quality of consciousness" that keeps your body relaxed and preserves the pleasure-oriented approach to your experience.

Your reading—as you will be frequently reminded—must be done *slowly*, as well as with the kinds of intentions and awareness just mentioned. You are asked, and will be asked again, to pause between sentences for a second or two, allowing time for what you have just been reading to sink in. Your brain has no previous experience of processing information presented in the way information is presented by NEUROSPEAK. Your central nervous system has no experience of receiving and passing along information in quite the way it is being asked to do it here. For your body, this is a learning experience, and the learning will be slower in the beginning than it will be once the entire process has become familiar.

Because you will be intending to read more slowly as well as more thoroughly than usual, you may have to be more than usually alert against tendencies to mind-wander, as well as tendencies to react to the novelty of the situation by holding your breath or tightening your muscles. Such tendencies can be very strong, and it is very important that you observe them and not allow yourself to engage in those behaviors. If you note that you are holding your breath, simply normalize your breathing and continue. If you notice that you have tightened your shoulders, simply release them, and so on. When you have done this repeatedly, you should be able to do your reading in a more relaxed way.

Similarly, after you have done a few of the exercises, it should be easier for you to use your consciousness as required, and it should also be easier for your body to assimilate and act upon the communications received.

Apart from the foregoing, any other needed instructions will be found in their appropriate places in the book. Paragraphs that ask you to perform physical actions or to make observations of your physical state or perceptions are set in italic type. Your reading and "doing" will be reinforced by information contained in the succeeding chapters.

4

FROM BRAIN TO FOOT

*N*ow, *as you read, let your feet rest flat-footed on the floor, and let them be parallel to one another—ten or twelve inches apart, whatever is comfortable. After finishing this sentence, just pay attention to both feet and notice how you sense your two feet—whether you sense them with clarity, how they make contact with the floor, and whatever else you may notice. I trust that you did that carefully without haste. If not—or in any case—do it once again, allowing at least one or two minutes for your observations. You **must** keep your feet about as they are now throughout the exercise.*

Now read on, just reading rather slowly and not bothering to try to make much sense of what is being said. Just know that one speaks differently when addressing the body as compared to addressing the mind, and your familiarity is with words addressing the mind. Therefore, at least until you have become accustomed to the differences and have gained some understanding of the method, what is said to you may seem strange and even rather pointless. Just allow for the possibility that a very interesting point will be made quite clear to you as you proceed.

I would like to remind you now that you have a right foot. If it is a typical, undamaged right foot, it has five toes. There is a right big toe and then another toe next to that one. Your right foot also has a middle toe and then a toe that corresponds to a ring finger. Your right foot also has a small toe. You may or may not know or be able to sense about your right foot which toe is longest, which toe is next in length, and next in length to that. But you will very probably know that the small toe of your right foot is the shortest one and that the big toe of your right foot is so-called because it is the one that is the largest in circumference. That big toe of your right foot is rather similar to the thumb of your right hand.

Your right foot resembles a hand in some other ways. For example, to the rear of the bones of the toes are other bones which go on back through your foot, and which help to support your right foot and give it flexibility as you move. Of course, you also have a right heel, and above that a right ankle that moves when the right foot is walking. There also is movement in your right ankle if you leave the ball of your right foot and your toes on the floor and simply raise your right heel.

You can probably raise your right toes all together and lower them. You can probably raise just your right big toe by itself. You can probably raise and lower the other four toes together. But, even though it is within your potential, you probably cannot move all the toes of your right foot in a differentiated way, similar to the way you are able to move your fingers.

You have seen your right foot many times. You have seen your right foot from above, from the inside, from the outside, and even from the bottom of your right foot. Your right foot has been with you throughout your life, and you really ought to know just what it looks like. But do you really know just what it looks like? Can you, without looking, visualize the toenails of your right foot, the spaces between your toes, the top of your right foot, your right ankle, and so on?

When you think about walking, do you really know just how your right foot moves? Do you come down on the heel of the right foot, then move along the bottom of the foot, coming up onto the ball of your right foot, and then the toes of your right foot leaving the floor in succession according to their lengths? What does it feel like as you put your foot down and walk on your foot, and pick it up again? Do you usually walk heavily or lightly with your right foot? Do you have any sense of how your right foot compares with walking on your other foot?

Do you know that you can just slide your right foot forward and backward? You can slide your right foot forward and backward many times. You can do it rather mindlessly, interested only in whether your right foot does slide forward and backward. Or you can do this movement intending to use your right foot to learn about the floor or carpet or whatever surface you are touching. You can also, with that same movement, deliberately use the surface you are touching to stimulate sensations in the bottom of your right foot. In fact, the bottom of your right foot, if properly stimulated, can provide you with real pleasure sensations. The end organs of touch on the bottom of the feet are some of the most sensitive to be found in a human body. Most probably, evolution intended this to protect you from injury.

However human beings in some cultures have so cultivated the sensitivity of the feet, and especially the bottom of the feet, as to treat the feet as a kind of secondary sexual organ. Your right foot could be stimulated to even that kind of pleasurable awareness.

You can also swivel the front of your right foot side to side. Your right heel can remain almost in place while the right foot travels well over to the left and then back over to the right, passing through the place where your right foot points out in front of you. Or, you could swivel your right foot so that your right heel moves from side to side, and the ball of your right foot stays more or less in place.

You can also make circles on the floor with your right foot. You can make small circles, or you can make big circles. You can make slow circles, or you can make quick circles. With your right foot, you can circle clockwise, or you can circle counterclockwise. You can also, with your right foot, combine some of those possibilities. For instance, you can make slow, small, clockwise circles, or you can make quick, large, counterclockwise circles with your right foot. Your right foot could make many combinations of movements, depending on the different possible sizes of the circles and how quickly or how slowly your right foot moves in one direction or the other.

Now, having read these remarks, please direct your awareness to your feet and observe whether they exist for you in the same way they existed for you before you began to read these statements about your right foot and some of its sensation and movement potentials. Is your awareness of your right foot the same as compared to your left foot? If not, what differences do you sense?

Can you sense the individual toes of your right foot somewhat more clearly? Does your right foot touch the floor somewhat differently?

Compare your sensing of your right lower leg with the left one, your right knee and your left one, your right shoulder and your left one. Compare the right side of your face with the left side. If you stop reading and close your eyes for a while, will you find that you are looking to the right? That possibly your head has turned spontaneously to the right—possibly even your whole upper body—so that your spine has twisted as it does when you twist to the right and your right shoulder has moved to the rear of the left one? It may be that you find yourself breathing—assuming there was no obstruction—more fully and clearly through your right nostril than through your left nostril.

In a moment, having finished this paragraph, get up and walk around the room and compare the way the right foot walks with the way the left foot walks—the contact with the floor, the foot's flexibility, whatever else you notice.

Do you begin to understand what is meant by the term NEUROSPEAK?

As you made your comparison, you probably noticed that not only did your right foot feel better, but that your left foot felt worse—stiff and lumpish, among other things. However, it is not true that your left foot is "worse" than before. Rather, your nervous system is comparing your left foot as it normally is with the improvements in your right foot, so the left one suffers by comparison.

It is good to allow those differences between the two feet to remain for a while. That encourages your body to adopt the superior organization and to move towards retaining it. It is also possible, as you will learn, to bring the left foot—or whatever body part it might be—very quickly to a condition similar to or identical with the improved part. It is also the case that you can do the same exercise over again, changing the wording from right to left, or left to right, as the case may be. Then you will get just the opposite effect from the one obtained by following the text—opposite in the sense that the opposite side will be the one to gain the benefits.

Do you begin to understand that writing for the body, and addressing the body, elicits responses very different from those which occur when the writing, like almost all writing, addresses the mind first of all?

Know and understand that this is only a beginning. ***As you read and as you learn—as you learn to respond and as you learn more about yourself in a variety of ways—deeper and more intricate changes will result. And, it may be that no part or function of your body is beyond the reach of words properly addressed.***

5

MOVEMENTS OF THE SHOULDER AND UPPER BACK

After reading this paragraph, please take the actions described and pay careful attention to your movements and sensations. At the end of the exercise, you will be asked to take the same actions and to compare your movements and sensations then with your movements and sensations as you will observe them in a moment. First, walk around the room and observe the movements in your shoulders as you walk and how you sense your shoulder movements. Also notice how your arms move as a result of your shoulder movements. After that, stand and sense your shoulders, comparing your right side with your left side. Take your arms back, and then overhead, and then to the front and down, making circles with your arms from your shoulders and comparing the ease of sensations of movements in your two shoulders. Then be seated and compare your awareness of your right and left shoulders, your right and left feet, the right and left sides of your pelvis, the right and left sides of your face, and your right and left sides as a whole. Please do that now.

Now sit with your feet flat on the floor, parallel to each other, ten to twelve inches apart. Try to position the rest of your body symmetrically and retain that symmetrical position of your body as you read on.

Your attention is called now to your right shoulder and right upper back, including your right shoulder blade. If you are able to sense them clearly, you may sense the top of your shoulder, the front of your shoulder, the outside of your shoulder, the back of your shoulder, and you may have some sense of your right shoulder joint and of how your right arm is attached to the right side of your body. You might also be aware of your right armpit and at what points your right upper arm is in contact with your right upper body.

Your right shoulder has many movement possibilities. You can, for example, move your right shoulder forward. You can move it forward and bring it back to its starting place, and move it forward and back again. Very definite sensations accompany those shoulder movements.

Were you to extend your right arm in front of you, you would discover that you can make a much more extensive forward movement with your right shoulder than you are able to do when your right hand is resting on your book, on your desk, on your thigh, or on your chair arm.

You can also move your right shoulder back, return it to its starting position, and repeat that movement many times. Then there are different, although somewhat similar sensations as compared to those which occur when your right shoulder is brought forward. If your right arm is behind you, then the shoulder movement back becomes much more extensive.

You will probably find that you can do a somewhat larger movement if you push up from your right shoulder joint, bringing your shoulder closer to your right ear and towards the ceiling. You can raise your right shoulder, lower it to its starting point, and raise and lower it while observing the sensations in your right shoulder. Were you to do a number of movements of your right shoulder—forward and back, then up and down—for any length of time, then you would almost certainly find that your right shoulder would hang lower than the other one. It would also feel more alive, as if it could move with greater ease and over a greater distance.

Your right shoulder can also be made to sink lower, and then come back up to its starting place. It can do this much better if your right arm is hanging at your side. Again, the sensations in your right shoulder will be different, although similar to the ones you are aware of when you move your right shoulder forward, or up, or back.

Now, you can also make circular movements with your right shoulder. You can move your right shoulder up, and then forward, and then down, and then back, and then up, and forward, and down, and back, and so on—circling and circling with your right shoulder. You can make small circles with your right shoulder, and you can make larger circles with your right shoulder. You can make slow circles with your right shoulder, and you can make faster ones. You can make small slow circles with your right shoulder, and you can make large quick circles with your right shoulder. You can make circles of different sizes and at different rates of movement.

You can also reverse the direction in which your right shoulder is circling. You can circle backwards for a while, and then you can circle forward for a while, sensing what you are doing with your right shoulder and what those movements feel like.

You could put the palm of your right hand on the thigh of your right leg, just a little above the knee. Then you could slide your right hand down your right leg, pushing with your right shoulder. And you could bring your right hand back up your leg by pulling with your right shoulder. Pushing and then pulling with your right shoulder, you could keep moving your right hand up and down your leg, all the way from your ankle to your hip joint, if you reach far enough. For that, you would need not only to push and pull from your right shoulder, but you would also have to allow your body to bend at the waist, moving forward and backward with your right shoulder.

You could also rest your right hand on top of your right shoulder with your upper arm at around shoulder height, and then make circles with your right arm, circling from your right shoulder. You could make all kinds of circles in this position, clockwise and counterclockwise, slow and fast, large and small—all kinds of combinations as your right shoulder circles with your right hand resting on that shoulder.

Also, with your right hand on your right shoulder, you could move your elbow forward so that your right shoulder rotates in. If you were to put your hand in your armpit, you would find that you would make a different shoulder movement and that the shoulder movement would be more towards the center of your body.

Also, that right shoulder movement towards the center of your body would grow larger as you placed your hand lower and lower on the right side of your body, until you finally reached a point of diminishing returns.

Something similar would happen if you placed your right hand on your right shoulder and moved your arm back behind you. Then your shoulder would move farther and farther back as your hand moved down your body until, once again, you reached a point of diminishing returns. The right shoulder movements would become smaller until finally there was almost no movement back by your shoulder or in your right shoulder blade or in the upper right side of your back.

Now, you could extend your right arm so that your right hand rests on the table in front of you, and you could make a light fist with your fingers. Then you could roll the fist like a wheel to the inside, feeling the rolling inward of your right shoulder. After that, you could roll the fist towards the outside of your body, feeling that your right shoulder rotates out. You can roll your fist from left to right, so that your right shoulder rotates in, and then out, and back again, experiencing a distinctly different sensation in your right shoulder and a different movement in your right shoulder than any previously described.

By this time, were you to do these movements, you would definitely find your right shoulder hanging lower than your left one. In fact, you would find that your pelvis has sunk lower on your right side, and that your whole body was tending to tilt to the right.

You would probably find that your head was cocked to the right, that your spine was curving to the right, and that, therefore, your rib cage was bending in towards the center of your body on your right side. You would probably also discover that your right hip joint had moved in such a way that your right knee was pointing off to the right, along with your right foot as well, while on your left side, your foot and knee would just be pointing forward.

In other words, you would discover that your nervous system was experiencing a very strong bias in favor of your right side. You would find that your right side felt at once less dense and more alive as compared to your left side. Especially you would be aware of feelings in your right shoulder that would probably include sensing down into your right shoulder joint when it is motionless and also if you were to decide to make circles or other movements with your right shoulder joint. And this sensing down into your shoulder on your right side would certainly be something very, very different from your experience of your shoulder on your left side, were you to compare the two shoulders as you just sit there.

Now, do notice how you are sitting and whether your nervous system is manifesting any bias towards your right side? Compare how you sense your right eye as compared to your left one. Close your eyes to make that—and other—comparisons. The right side of your lips as compared to the left side. The right side of your face as compared to the left side. Your right shoulder as compared to your left shoulder.

Now, physically, objectively, circle for a moment with your two shoulders and compare. Compare not only your shoulder movements but also what you sense to be happening in the upper back on your right side and your left side.

Next get up and just walk around, comparing your right side with your left side—first of all, how your shoulders and arms move, then whatever else you notice, including the contact with the floor that is being made by your right foot and your left foot.

After that, stop and make some large circles overhead with your right and left arms. Do simultaneous circles and also do alternating circles. Do circles that begin by your arms moving back, and circles that begin by your arms moving forward. Then stand and compare your two shoulders and arms. After that return to your chair, and make any other observations you can.

6

REORGANIZING THE BODY'S RELATIONSHIP TO GRAVITY

*First, just read this paragraph. Then do as you are instructed. As you follow the instructions, **be as observant as possible of your sensations and movements, intending to remember exactly what you observe**, so that you can compare your present condition with what you experience when you have completed the exercise. You will observe, first of all, how you stand and what it feels like. Notice your sensations of the length—or height—of your body, the contact of your feet with the floor, how your upper body feels—including especially your lower back—and how you hold your head. Notice whether your head feels erect, so that you look out towards the horizon rather than down towards the floor or up towards the ceiling. Try to be aware as well of what you do with your eyes—whether they look out towards the horizon, or whether they look down, or up, or off towards one side. Then, still carefully observing yourself, walk around and make similar observations, including sensations of both the height and the weight of your body. Perform those actions now and then return to your chair.*

Now, just as you have done it before, be seated with both of your feet resting flat on the floor. Your feet should be—and should remain—parallel to one another, about ten or twelve inches apart.

Remember, it is critically important that you read slowly and with a strong focus of attention. Pause for a second or two between each sentence in order that NEUROSPEAK may have its full potential impact on your brain and central nervous system. Then, as you have experienced before, your muscles and skeleton will be able to assimilate the signals which they require to reorganize involuntarily as a result of your reading.

If your feet are normal ones, they have toes and bones with joints inside the toes. At the bottoms of your toes, your foot becomes one fleshy mass, and inside that mass, there are other, longer bones which extend through your feet and on back towards your heels. Your heels also have bones, but bones quite different in appearance from those bones inside your toes and inside the larger parts of your feet.

Just above your heel, of course, is your ankle. Your ankle has its own fairly complicated bony structure and, above that, are the long bones of your lower legs. Those bones and the rest of your lower legs exist between your ankles and your knees. Those lower legs are much longer than your feet, *extending quite some distance up your body* from your ankles to your knees.

Your knees have their own fairly complicated structure and a larger range of movement than your ankles. In part, this is required because not only are your legs below your knees quite long, but your legs above your knees are also quite long. Your legs above your knees, including your thighs, are probably a good bit more sensitive to your touch than your lower legs and calves are. In fact, if you draw your fingers up the upper part of your legs, pressing a little into your flesh with your fingernails, you are likely to find that the sensations are stronger—and probably quite a bit more pleasurable—as you move up your thighs towards your pelvis and your buttocks.

At the front of your body, there is your pubic region, your lower belly and then—*as your consciousness moves up your body*—there is your navel. To the rear of your navel is the lower segment of your spine. Your spine proceeds from your tail bone, anchored to your pelvis, on up through your body, and is composed of many vertebrae of differing sizes. Then, there is the region you refer to as your waist and, just above that, your ribs.

Hanging somewhat lower than your waist and ribs are your hands and fingers. They are somewhat similar to your toes and feet, just as your wrists and your arms have considerable similarity to your ankles and legs. Above your wrists are what you call your forearms, leading on up to your elbows. You can doubtless sense that your ribs begin somewhere near the place—in terms of height—where your lower arms join your elbows. Then there are your upper arms and, at the uppermost ends of them, your shoulder joints and shoulders.

Your ribs—and your ribcage—surround much of your upper body, protecting a number of vital organs. You have many ribs, *and as your consciousness moves up your body towards your chest and your armpits*, it should be possible to feel that your ribs move gently out and in, in concert with your breathing. If your sensing is accurate, you will experience the movements of your ribs to some extent in the front of your body, but more in your sides and in your back.

The chest and breasts are usually rather clearly sensed. Your awareness of your breasts will be at different levels of your body depending on their size and shape. Just above your breast bone, and out to the sides, are your shoulders. You also have shoulder joints, and you may also be aware of your shoulder blades. Your spine rises even beyond the tops of your shoulders and up into your neck, up behind your jaw bones and into the base of your skull.

Inside your neck is not only your spine but also your throat, of which you become aware, if you are not aware of it otherwise, when you are eating or drinking. At the same time as you are aware of your throat, you are also likely to be aware of the interior of your mouth and, perhaps, of your jaws.

Your awareness of the interior of your mouth quite likely includes the floor and the roof of your mouth, the sides of your mouth, your teeth, and your tongue. Of all the parts of the human body, usually none are experienced so clearly as are the lips. The lips are sensed with such clarity because they are involved in activities of very great importance both for survival and for meeting fundamental and powerful emotional needs—taking in food, communicating with other people through speech, and making love. You may notice even now as you are reading how clear your own lips are in your body image—your body as you are able to sense it.

Above your lips are other parts of your body which are very important. There is your nose, necessary for breathing and also for your sense of smell. There are your ears, necessary for your hearing. And there are your eyes, without which you would have no visual knowledge of your world and, also without which you would have a very different way of imagining and of remembering.

Because of the great importance of those parts of your body located in your head, usually your face and your head as a whole are quite clearly sensed as compared to most other body parts. The remainder of the exterior of your head—your forehead and those parts of the head that are in most cases covered with hair—are also fairly clearly sensed, but probably not so clearly as you sense your face. That is partly because the flesh is not very thick or sensitive as it fits over the exterior of your skull.

Your skull provides a place and protection for the most important single part of the human body—the brain. Other parts may be as important for sustaining life, but no other part is as important for the way your life is lived.

Within your skull, your brain—which you do not sense—is divided into two hemispheres, each one an enormously complicated structure that is characterized by constant electrical and chemical activities. Visible from the top of your brain is the so-called cerebral divide, or corpus collosum. While it is taught that you cannot sense your brain, nonetheless it is true that when consciousness is kept focused for a while on the brain space, then there is a feeling that the brain is being sensed, sometimes quite vividly. Whether the focus creates an image of the brain, or just why that sensation is experienced, is not altogether clear.

Your focus on your brain space can be easily maintained when you have the feeling that your eyes are looking up into your brain space and circling in that space. You can have the feeling that your eyes are making horizontal circles, vertical circles, diagonal circles, all kinds of circles, circling in different directions, in your brain space.

You can also have the sense of breathing up into your brain space. You can have the feeling of directing your breathing into your brain's left hemisphere, or into your brain's right hemisphere, or up into and beyond that cerebral divide between your hemispheres. You can feel that you breathe *up through your brain, up into the top of your skull, and even beyond that.* You can feel that you breathe up through your brain space and into your skull in such a manner that your skull elongates as you breathe up through it. Or you can feel that you breathe right up through the top of your skull and that your breath then extends beyond the top of your skull. Your breath moving up through your brain and the top of your skull, higher and higher, however far up through the top of your head and beyond it that you might choose to breathe. Just allow yourself several seconds to assimilate what has been said to you.

Now, when you have completed reading this paragraph, stand and observe how you stand and compare that with what you experienced before you began to read through this exercise. Then walk around and compare what you experience as you walk now with what you experienced when you observed your walking at the beginning of this chapter of the book. After that, come back to your chair and read the concluding paragraph. Make these observations now.

What did you observe? What about feelings of length or height, and the way your body was supported, your upper body especially? How did you hold your head and where did your eyes look? What about feelings of weight, or lightness, and the kind of contact your feet made with the floor as you walked? Did your head feel somewhat as if it was floating in space as you moved? Sometimes it even happens that when the body is experienced as elevated, the emotions or mood may be experienced as elevated also. Does any of this describe what you have experienced? What else have you to add? Walk around a little more if you feel that you may have missed something.

7

A Hand To Touch With/A Hand To Be Touched By

As you have observed, when you have completed any NEUROSPEAK exercise, you are able to sense more clearly and you are able to move more efficiently whatever part of your body you have been reading about. As you do more of these exercises, it becomes more and more likely that the changes brought about will be permanent ones, and also that additional benefits will be realized. The potential for genius-level functioning is present in every human brain, and it could be actualized if only the brain were sufficiently and effectively used. Reading this book is not likely to actualize your potential to such an extent, but it does move you in that direction. The exercises have the effect of freeing or disinhibiting brain cells "frozen" in your motor cortex. More of your brain becomes more active, not only in your motor cortex but also in adjacent parts of your brain which have to do with thinking and feeling functions.

The effects are cumulative as the "work" progresses. Not only do you improve the condition of your brain, and use your brain better, but you also cumulatively improve your body image—that is, sensing your body more clearly and also more accurately. As this occurs, you know more exactly just what it is that you are doing. You then become less awkward, less wasteful of your energy resources, and less prone to accidental injury. Your body becomes less inclined to retain those muscular patterns resulting from psychological and emotional stress so that, in fact, you are less susceptible to "being stressed." As your sensing improves and as your use of your body improves, you will also be considerably less vulnerable to those symptoms of bodily misuse which are often mistakenly attributed to aging. For practical purposes, you will age more slowly and more gracefully than you would if you failed to increase your awareness and to use your body in the light of this awareness.

Brief as this book is, and despite the fact that it enables you to "work" with only a few parts of your body, it can definitely—and beneficially—change you. It will open you to the possibility both of a larger awareness and of using a body with much greater potential for moving, sensing, and experiencing pleasure than you previously recognized. Then you could go on to develop those possibilities further and gain still greater benefits. But you can do nothing until you have been shown the way, and that is what is happening to you now as you read and "do" this book.

Perhaps by now you are accustomed to approaching each exercise by sitting with your feet flat on the floor, parallel to each other and about ten to twelve inches apart. You have been requested to sit in such a way that your movements as you read will be minimal. In the case of the present chapter, we have a slight problem that we have not encountered before. You are going to be reading about your left hand and that reading will effect various *changes in your experience of your left hand and of your left hand's ability to sense and to move. However, you must also use your hands to hold your book or at least to turn the pages of your book. Therefore, try to minimize your awareness of using your hands to touch the book or other objects around you and allow any awareness of your left hand to be determined as fully as possible **just by the words you are reading.***

At the end of this paragraph, you should carry out the actions described. This will provide you with a basis for comparing your hand as it presently is with your hand as it will be. For a moment now, look at your hands as they rest parallel to each other with the palms down and lying in as identical positions as possible. Notice everything you can about the appearance of your hands and compare them. Then explore your left thigh and knee with your left hand, noticing what and how you sense. After that, do the same with your right hand and your right leg and knee. Also use your left hand to explore your right hand and arm and then your right elbow as you flex and extend your right arm to enable your left hand to sense your elbow as it moves. Then use your right hand to sense your left hand and arm and then your left elbow as it moves. After that, position your hands as symmetrically as possible. Do these actions now and then proceed to the next paragraph.

Remember that what we are doing is still unfamiliar to your brain, although your brain is certainly learning. Eventually, when your brain has become more experienced, it will surely function more quickly. But for now, as you have been instructed before, it is necessary for you to read slowly and carefully and to maintain the focus of your consciousness on what you are reading. Again, it will be helpful if you pause for a second or two at the end of each sentence, providing a little extra time for the words to sink in and be acted upon.

Now we are going to discuss in some detail your left hand. That hand begins at your wrist, and it has bones inside of the hand that extend on up towards the bottoms or bases of your fingers. The palm of your left hand is very richly endowed with nerve endings which enable your left hand to touch with great sensitivity. The top of your left hand is much less sensitive. It is not required to be as sensitive as your left palm since it is not often used for touching, either to learn about whatever your left hand is touching or to provide another body with sensations.

Similarly, the undersides of the fingers of your left hand are more sensitive than the tops. The insides of your fingers are more sensitive than the tops of your fingers, but less sensitive than the bottoms. Your left hand has, of course, five fingers. Or, if you prefer, it has four left fingers and a left thumb. You can probably sense that your thumb is larger in circumference than your other fingers are, especially your left small finger. You may also be able to sense the comparative lengths of the fingers of your left hand and to sense clearly that your left middle finger is the longest one.

Unless you bring the fingers of your left hand together, there are spaces between them. The spaces between the fingers on either side of your middle finger are quite probably almost identical. The space between your small finger and your left ring finger is probably, however, different from the space between your left forefinger and your left thumb.

You can easily sense the joints in the fingers of your left hand by bringing the fingers into a fist and then extending them again, and you could do this repeatedly, flexing and extending them quickly, and flexing and extending them slowly. You can also raise and lower your fingers, all of them at once or separately, as you might do if you were playing a piano with your left hand and fingers.

Because of the amount of movement regularly done, the left hand of a pianist is likely to be agile and sensitive. You can doubtless imagine how your left hand would move if you regularly played the piano as a concert pianist. Your left hand might also be extremely sensitive, and perhaps also extremely agile, if you used it regularly to work on other people's bodies as some kinds of healers do. Your left hand then would touch not only the surface of another body but would feel down into it, touching far more deeply and completely than hands ordinarily do. You could have that kind of left hand.

You could begin to have such a sensitive hand by moving it up and down your left leg and using it to sense as completely as possible your left leg as you touch it. You could use your left hand to explore your left knee, trying to touch as completely as possible the bones of your knee with your left hand. Then, if you would bend and straighten your left leg, you could sense what was happening in your left knee still more completely.

There are many things you can do which will tend to increase the sensitivity of your left hand, to make your left hand more vivid in your body image, and also to improve the functioning of your left hand in a variety of other ways. Improvement occurs, for example, when consciousness remains focused on even very simple activities. You can, for example, leave the top parts of your three middle fingers on the table while you rap on the table with the heel of your left hand. You might rap with the heel of your left hand in rhythmic bursts of one and two and three and four raps. Alternatively, you could leave the heel of your hand on the table and rap with the palm and fingers of your left hand in rhythmic bursts of one and two and three and four raps. You could leave the heel of your hand in place and slide the fingers of your left hand side to side. Or you can leave your fingers in place and slide the heel and the palm of your left hand side to side. You can also simply slide your left hand forward and back or you can take the left hand side to side, sliding it across the table or some other surface. Or you might make circles on the table with the palm of your hand, circling in a clockwise direction, and then in a counterclockwise direction. With your left hand, you can make circles that are small, and you can make circles that are large. You can make fast circles, and you can make slow circles. You can make all kinds of circles, with different variations of slow and fast, large and small, clockwise and counterclockwise, always circling and sensing with your left hand.

You have probably had the experience of leaving your left hand in very cold water for a while, so that the hand becomes increasingly numb the longer it stays in the water. Your left hand also knows what hot water feels like. Your left hand knows what it is like to touch or hold ice. It also knows what it is like to touch or hold something hot.

Your left hand knows what fur feels like—what fur feels like to the palm of your hand and to the back of your hand and what fur feels like between the fingers of your left hand. Your left hand knows what feathers feel like, and also what leather feels like, and plain cotton fabric. Your left hand has probably touched velvet, and it knows what satin feels like, and also silk. Your left hand knows what it is like to touch the bark of a tree, or a leaf, or grass. Your left hand knows what sandpaper feels like, and wet glass, and polished wood. Your left hand can recall what it feels like to shape itself around pieces of metal. Your left hand knows what it feels like to touch human flesh and how many different experiences are possible for your left hand to have just within the context of touching human flesh.

You can use your left hand to learn about the surfaces it is touching, but you can also use most surfaces to stimulate sensations in your left hand. Again, your left hand, your palm and the undersides of your fingers are extremely richly endowed with nerve endings for touching. Because of this fact, it is also possible to highly stimulate those parts of your left hand, so that the hand becomes extremely sensitive and also highly energized. It is that energy in your left hand that another person might experience as heat if, for example, you were doing healing work. So much energy could be transmitted by your left hand that the heat would feel almost as if it could burn your body or someone else's body.

When the situation is appropriate, your left hand can take in, and also transmit, what will clearly be felt to be sexual energy. The palm of the hand and the fingers can become so energized as to feel at least mildly orgasmic, and then your hand could awaken similar sensations in almost any part of another person's body, when your hand touched that body caressingly.

Once you have experienced such a possibility, you can use other surfaces to awaken different kinds of sensitivities and different kinds of energies in your left hand. Whether those are, for example, healing or sexual energies, or other kinds of energies, your hand can become so sensitized that it no longer feels quite solid, but rather as if it is composed of particles of energy flowing or dancing. When your left hand is so energized, the energy will be experienced throughout your left hand and not just by your palm and the undersides of your fingers.

When your left hand has achieved that kind of subtlety and sensitization, then it can truly sense deeply into other bodies, and it can also feed its energies deeply into other bodies. *Your left hand can be like that.*

Now, at the end of the next two paragraphs, you will please do the following, preferably with your eyes closed. First, compare your awareness of your left hand with your awareness of your right hand. You should also compare your awareness of your left shoulder with your right one and notice how the left side of your pelvis sits as compared to the right side and how your left foot is sensed and relates to the floor as compared to your right one. Then use the palm and undersides of the fingers of your left hand to explore your left leg and knee. After that, use your right hand to explore your right leg and knee and compare those two experiences. Also touch and explore your right hand with your left one, and then use your right hand to touch and explore your left one and observe how differently your right hand touches than your left hand does. Your left hand will almost certainly touch in a way that elicits feelings of refinement and yields more knowledge as compared to the touching your right hand is able to do. Your right hand exploring your left hand, however, will touch something that is more subtle than itself.

Let your right elbow rest in the palm of your left hand, and then flex and extend your right arm, sensing the elbow with your left hand. Then let your right hand sense your left elbow as you flex and extend your left arm. Compare those two experiences. After that, get up and walk around and compare your awareness of your left hand and arm with your right one. Then, use your left hand in other ways to explore further how your hand can experience what it touches when it has been brought somewhat closer to its sensitivity potentials.

8

A Tongue for All Seasons and All Reasons

Once again, just be seated as before comfortably in the same kind of chair, and let your feet rest flat on the floor, parallel to each other, about ten to twelve inches apart. Make as certain as you can that you will not be interrupted or otherwise distracted, and remember that as you read, the quality of consciousness you bring to your reading—your concentrated focus as you read slowly and carefully—will, more than anything else, determine how much you will benefit from the exercise. Now, when you are asked to do so, make your observations as instructed so that you can compare your condition at present with what you sense and do at the conclusion of your work.

First, however, it should be mentioned that it is very common for the muscles of the **tongue** to be habitually tensed or over-contracted. Such chronic tension in the tongue has many unfortunate consequences—among them, the head and neck cannot turn as freely as they should, eye movements are inhibited and the eyes may become strained, and there is likely to be some interference with speech and with breathing. In some cases, movements of the mouth are affected, including proper eating and drinking. Tension in the tongue may contribute to tension in the jaw, to dental problems, and to headaches. Even movements of the spine in the upper and lower back may become impaired as an end result of chronic tension in the tongue.

When the tongue is free, it lies wide and flat in the mouth, and the tip of the tongue protrudes very slightly between the upper and lower teeth. The tongue, when sufficiently free, will move in coordination with movements of the eyes, neck, and head. If the eyes go right, the tongue will go right. If the head turns right, the tongue will move right, as will the eyes if there is no inhibition of the eye movements to prevent it. Similarly, the tongue and eyes will coordinate with the head and neck in the case of up and down movements or any other head and neck movements for that matter.

What this kind of **coordination** means is that the tongue will move even in the direction of thought or attention. If a person is thinking of something off to her right, then her tongue will involuntarily move into the right side of her mouth. If a person is thinking about or attending to something off to his left, then his tongue will quite involuntarily—and, typically, quite unconsciously—move over to the left side of his mouth. That is what happens when the body moves as it ought to. The reason those movements occur is that the head and eyes will always tend to move in the direction being thought about or attended to. The muscular movements in the neck and the eyes may be very small ones, but they are sufficient to produce the larger movement of the tongue which will bring it into the right or left side of the mouth, or the roof or floor of the mouth, as appropriate.

Now, take a minute or two and observe how your tongue is lying and what it does when you turn your head right and left or just move *your eyes right and left. If your tongue does not move with your head and eye movements, then not only is your tongue chronically tensed, but it is impairing your head and eye movements. If your tongue does move with your head and eyes, then just hold it fixed in the middle of your mouth and you will quickly become aware of how this holding strains your eyes and impedes the turning of your head and neck as you move your head from left to right and back again a few times.*

If your tongue remains in the middle of your mouth when you move your head and eyes side to side, then try opposing the movements of your tongue to the movements of your head and eyes—your tongue going left when your head and eyes go right. This will make you aware of the interrelationship between your tongue, your eyes, and the muscles of your neck.

Also observe whether it feels to you as if your tongue lies wide and flat, whether the tip of your tongue extends a bit into the space between your upper and lower teeth, and to what extent it seems to you that you are sensing the whole surface of your tongue, and perhaps beyond the surface. Turn your head left to right a few times just to get a sense of what that feels like, how easily it turns, and how quickly it will turn without any sense of straining or forcing. Now take your tongue from side to side in your mouth, observing those movements and how they are affected if you open your mouth slightly, then a little more, and a little more, until you reach a point when the movements of your tongue are no longer helped by your mouth being open, but the tongue begins to feel obstructed by the tensions in your mouth and jaw when you force the opening wider than is comfortable. And now, just read—slowly, carefully, pausing as usual between sentences.

Unless the tongue is being actively and *voluntarily* used, or unless it is being looked at or otherwise deliberately sensed, most people have little or no awareness of it. They do not know how it lies in the mouth, or how it should lie if it is well organized. They do not know if it moves with the eyes and the head, or that it ought to do so. The truth about those facts, as about so many basic facts of everyday use of the body, is simply unknown to the point that there is no awareness even of *not knowing* things that a healthy and adequately functioning organism would know.

Even when you observe your tongue in the mirror, you are not likely to look to see how it normally lies—whether it lies wide and flat, or whether it looks contracted and rounded. Nor are you likely to look to see whether your tongue, in its resting position, has the tip between your upper and lower teeth or is to the rear of your teeth.

If you choose to pay enough attention to your tongue, you may, however, find yourself becoming increasingly aware of its surface—the top of your tongue, the sides of your tongue, and the bottom or underside of your tongue. You may then become aware of its length, and of feelings of wetness and perhaps of heat in your tongue. You are likely to sense more wetness on the underside of your tongue than on top. Paying sufficient attention to your tongue—bringing it at least for a time into your body image—is likely to make it feel bigger.

As you were asked to observe, the range and agility of your tongue's movement capacities may be partly observed by moving it left to right inside your mouth. If you do that with your mouth closed, the tongue movements will be small, and you will likely feel that the base of your tongue where the movements originate is being blocked from making larger movements. Then, as the mouth is opened more and more, your tongue can move more and with greater freedom and ease of movement—up to the point when strain is felt in the jaw as it forces the mouth to open wider than is comfortable. Then you will once again sense that your tongue movements are limited and blocked, although for different reasons.

Your tongue can be used to explore the interior of your mouth in many different ways. For example, your tongue can roam around the roof of your mouth and discover that the roof of your mouth is quite sensitive to your tongue's touch and may even be quite ticklish. You may discover that your tongue has much more space to roam around in as it explores the roof of your mouth than it has when it is exploring the floor of your mouth.

When your tongue explores the interior of your left cheek, then it will touch a quite different kind of surface and it will also have quite a lot of space to explore. Unlike the roof or the floor of your mouth, the sides of your mouth are much softer and much more yielding. Your left cheek, for example, is very soft comparatively, and it will easily stretch and yield as your tongue pushes against its interior. The same is true, of course, for the right side of your mouth should you choose to explore it with your tongue.

Your tongue can have quite a rich and varied experience as it explores, one by one, the backs of your lower teeth. Your tongue can also explore the tops, the biting edges of your lower teeth. And, one by one, it can explore the front of your lower teeth, finding that the sensations are very different depending on whether your tongue is exploring the front, or the back, or the biting edge surfaces of your teeth.

And it is a significantly different experience to use your tongue to explore the back of your upper teeth, and then the front of your upper teeth, exploring your teeth one by one with your tongue, and then taking your tongue side to side across your upper teeth so that it moves somewhat in the manner that a wiper moves across a windshield of a car.

You can also move your tongue back and forth, left to right, so that the bottom of your tongue passes over the biting edge of your lower teeth, while the top of your tongue simultaneously passes over the biting edge of your upper teeth.

You can also, simultaneously, explore the inside of your upper lip and the outside of your upper teeth with your tongue. In the same way, your tongue can explore the inside of your lower lip and the outside of your lower teeth, both at the same time. And you can use your tongue to move back and forth so that it first moves across your upper lip and your upper teeth, then your lower lip and your lower teeth, making an oval shape as it moves. You can even do this action in such a way that when your tongue moves left, it continues on into the left side of your cheek, and when your tongue moves right, it continues on into the right side of your cheek.

You can draw your tongue back so that the tip of your tongue is some distance to the rear of your teeth, and you can practice retracting your tongue and then bringing it forward just to the point where it makes contact with the backs of your teeth. Or you can take your tongue back as far as it is possible to do without straining, and then bring it forward so that it extends between your teeth and between your lips and sticks out visibly in front of you. You can retract your tongue and extend it in that way many times, taking it back as far as it will easily go, then pushing it forward as far as it will go without feeling forced.

You can lengthen and release your tongue quite measurably if you place the tip of your tongue between your teeth and then bite down on your tongue very gently. Then push your tongue forward a little bit more and bite down on it gently again and again and again, each time pushing your tongue a little further out, then biting down on it gently to mark your progress. As you continue doing this, repeating the process of extending your tongue in small increments, you may find that you can take thirty or forty such little bites before your tongue is as far out of your mouth as you can push it. Then, as you repeat the process some more, you may become able to take fifty bites, or sixty, your tongue coming further and further out of your mouth, as your brain responds to the message it is receiving by enabling your tongue to lengthen more and more. After you have continued with these movements for a while, your tongue may in fact be quite noticeably longer than it was when you began. When you take it back into your mouth and let it rest there, your tongue may be sensed to lie flatter and wider. It may also protrude a bit farther between your teeth than you would want to have it, but it will quickly reorganize to move back into its proper position, the tip extending just very slightly between your teeth.

What your tongue feels and how you feel your tongue can vary a great deal depending upon the orientation and intention you bring to the use of your tongue. For example, you can use your tongue to sense the surfaces your tongue is touching, doing this in order to learn about those surfaces, as your tongue is able by its sensing to reveal to you what those surfaces are like. But you might also use your tongue with a different intention as you move it over those same surfaces, and while touching the surfaces in what will appear to be an almost identical way, have the intention of learning how your tongue *responds* to the surfaces—learning not about what your tongue is touching but rather about your tongue's sensations as it touches.

You can also vary your approach, and thereby your experience, in some other basic ways. For example, you can deliberately use your tongue to stimulate sensations in whatever part of your mouth or lips or other body part your tongue may be touching. Or you can deliberately use whatever parts your tongue is touching in order to stimulate sensations in your tongue. The experience will be very different in each case—both for your tongue and for what your tongue touches. (Should you touch with your tongue some part of another person's body, varying just *your* intentions, it will be the case that the person's experience as well as your own will be quite different, depending on what your *intention* is.)

There are many other variations which might be introduced as you explore the movement and sensory potentials of your tongue. For example, you can use your tongue *to stimulate* the interior of your left cheek while, simultaneously, using your tongue *to learn about* the interior surface of your cheek. Or you could focus your awareness on what your lower lip is feeling while you are touching your lower lip with your tongue and while you are, at the same time, making use of your lower lip to stimulate sensations in your tongue. In these cases, you must divide your consciousness, and you may then discover that you have also divided the quantity and intensity of your sensations. You might also find yourself able to allocate different portions of the available sensations to your tongue, to your cheek, or to any other parts your tongue might touch. You might intend—and achieve—in other words, that your tongue take three-fourths of the available sensation, leaving one-fourth to your (ordinarily much more sensitive) lips.

After your tongue has been given all of these experiences, and if they have been done with awareness and in a leisurely manner, your tongue is quite likely to move more freely and quickly than it moved before and to coordinate more efficiently and gracefully with the movements of your eyes, head, and neck. Your tongue will probably move more quickly from side to side if you deliberately move your eyes and tongue together left to right, or if you turn your head left to right and move your tongue and your eyes from left to right, finding out how quickly you can do that. You will likely also find that your head and neck turn more easily and smoothly from side to side, so that you will know in that way that your neck muscles have released.

Then, if the exercise has been sufficiently successful, you should find that you only have to turn your head left to right to be aware that your tongue moves spontaneously with your head. And you may only have to move your eyes left to right to discover that your tongue moves with your eyes. If your tongue already was coordinated, then perhaps the quality of the tongue movements will be recognized by you as being better.

You may even only need to think about something happening at some distance from the left side of your head to observe that your tongue spontaneously moves over to the left side of your mouth. You may only have to imagine something happening well over to your right side in order to observe that your tongue has moved over towards or into your right cheek, and you may also find that your tongue moves up and down according to whether you imagine something happening well above your head or pay attention to something happening down around or below your feet.

Now, make those observations, beginning with how your tongue lies in your mouth, and then noting how it coordinates with head and eye movements and with where you focus your attention. And notice how clearly you are aware now of the surfaces of your tongue. Turn your head very quickly side to side, taking note of how your head is moving. Also, with your mouth opened short of straining, take your tongue side to side and notice whether that movement has improved. Sit quietly, with your eyes closed, and try to make some further observations.

9

LEARNING ACROSS THE HEMISPHERES

As you usually do, read this paragraph and then carry out the actions described to provide you with a basis for recognizing the changes in your body which have been made by NEUROSPEAK. The human body, while not often sensed very well, is usually sensed as being symmetrical. That is, the average person senses with about equal clarity his or her right and left legs, right and left arms, right and left shoulders, the two sides of the face, and so on. The body typically is felt as weighing about the same on each side, and the two sides are experienced also as being about equal in length. That is what is meant here by **symmetry**.

Now, get up and stand with your two feet facing out at equal angles and your two arms hanging in a similar way. Notice whether your body feels symmetrical in terms of clarity of sensing, weight, and length. Then walk around and make the same observations. After that, return to your chair, and in a seated position, scan your body for symmetry. Then read on, slowly and carefully, pausing a second or two between sentences. Remember, this type of processing is new for your brain, something that has to be learned before your brain can function quickly while doing it.

You should sit, as you usually do, with your two feet parallel to each other and about ten or twelve inches apart. Maintain that position and also try to maintain an approximately symmetrical positioning of the rest of your body.

You will probably feel that your two buttocks and the bottoms of your two feet rest symmetrically on your chair and on the floor.

Now I would like to call your attention to the fact that your right foot is resting on the floor with your right lower leg at approximately a right angle to your right foot. Your right upper leg is at approximately a right angle to your right lower leg. And, if you are seated erect, then the right side of your upper body is at about a right angle to your right upper leg.

You know that you could move your right foot in any number of ways. You could keep your right heel on the floor and then rap on the floor with the ball of your right foot. You could rap with the ball of your right foot in bursts of one and two and three and four raps, or you could rap with your right foot without any discernible pattern.

Leaving your right heel more or less in place, you could swivel the front part of your right foot side to side, your right foot all the while keeping contact with the floor. Or, you could slide your right heel side to side, the front part of your right foot remaining more or less in place. You could also move your right ankle in such a way that you could go onto the outside and then onto the inside of your right foot, and you could do that many times.

You could extend your right leg and, allowing your heel to rest on the floor, make circles in the air with your right foot. You could also wriggle your toes. Having extended your leg, you could bring it back towards you again, using the joint of your right knee. You could flex and extend your right leg many times, using the muscles that serve to move your leg from the knee joint.

You could run your right hand up and down your right leg sensing the front and back and sides of your right leg with your right hand. You could put your hand in several different kinds of relationship to your right leg. Your right hand could be used to explore and study your right lower leg, intending to learn as much about it as possible. You could use your right hand to stimulate many different kinds of sensations in your right lower leg and right knee. You could also use your right lower leg and knee to stimulate sensations in your right hand. And there are other possibilities. It all depends on the intentions you bring to the sensory mechanisms of your right hand.

Of course, you could do the same with your right upper leg. You could move your hand over your right thigh, for example, in such a way as to stimulate strong sensations in the palm of your hand and in the undersides of your right fingers. You could use the fingers and fingernails of your right hand to dig into your right upper leg in ways that would stimulate pleasurable sensations which could be quite intense. You could bend your right arm at the elbow and then use your right hand to slap your right upper leg or, perhaps, to rap on it rhythmically in bursts of one and two and three and four raps.

You could bend your right elbow and then make circles in the air with your right arm and hand, circling from your elbow. You could also rest your right hand on the right side of your rib cage and make circles with your elbow, but this time circling from your right shoulder joint. Or you could circle from your right shoulder by just extending your right arm out in front of you and circling, or by extending your right arm overhead and circling from the shoulder.

You could also, of course, use different parts of the right side of your body to experience the world outside of yourself. You could touch different parts of your chair with your right hand, using your hand to learn about the chair, or using the chair to stimulate sensations in your right hand. You can press your right leg, or your right arm against parts of the chair, stimulating sensations in those parts of your right side. You could also simply pay attention to how your right buttock is resting on your chair and what you experience as being the position of the right side of your pelvis.

You can explore the interior of the right side of your mouth with your tongue, gliding your tongue along, rapping with your tongue against the inside of your cheek, or pushing against your right cheek. You can focus your breathing on your right nostril, so that you are aware of breathing just on your right side. Then you may notice movement in your ribs on your right side and that your right shoulder rises and falls as you inhale and exhale through the right side of your nose. You can make blinking movements with your right eye—possibly in rhythmic bursts of one and two and three and four blinks.

Your consciousness has the ability to move up and down the whole length of the right side of your body, moving slowly from the bottom of your right foot all the way up your right side to the top of your head. Then, from the right side of the top of your head, it can move down over the right side of your face, sensing the face, and then down the right side of your neck, your right shoulder, your right upper body and arm and hand, the right side of your pelvis, your right leg and right foot, and then roam back up and down, just sensing the right side of your body many times.

After reading this paragraph, you will begin more observations. This time, however, you can begin them while still sitting. Notice, for example, whether the whole right side of your body feels to you to be lower than the left side—your pelvis sinking lower into your chair, your shoulder held lower, your right foot making a more complete contact with the floor. Pay attention also to whether you sense your right eye more clearly than your left eye, your right shoulder more clearly than your left one, your right upper leg more clearly, and so on. Then get up and stand and make similar observations. After that, walk around and once again pay attention to your body's symmetry—or, as it now is, asymmetry—with partial reference to the clarity of sensing between the two sides as well as sensations of weight and length. Walk very quickly and note if the asymmetry becomes still more evident.

If you paid close attention, you almost certainly had a quite clear sensation that your body was longer on the right side. You should have sensed that it moved more freely on the right side, that it seemed more energetic and alive, and that your right foot made a better contact with the floor. There are also many other changes you may have noticed—including perhaps different breathing on the right side, a greater clarity of vision on your right side, a tendency to look to the right, and still others. Try observing once more—sitting, then standing, and after that, walking, and observe very closely and just as thoroughly as you can as many differences as you can between the organization and the functioning of your right and left sides. When you are finished, come back and be seated, and we will take this process a step further.

As it has been explained to you, there are advantages in leaving the side "worked on" in its altered and improved condition. Your nervous system, if reasonably healthy, is both rational and hedonistic. That is to say, it is inclined to seek pleasure and to avoid pain. Thus, when one side of your body has been enabled to feel better and to move better, your nervous system will want to preserve that more pleasurable way of being. The longer it is able to observe the more pleasurable way of being, the greater the chances that it will strive to make the changes permanent, either by retaining them or by making efforts to regain them.

There is also another possibility—transferring what has been learned on one side of the body quickly over to the other side. In the case of NEUROSPEAK, in which changes are achieved simply by reading, such transference is less easy to do than when actual movements, or movements reinforced by sensory images, are used. Nonetheless, we will attempt such a transference now, and we should achieve at the least a restoration of your body's symmetry at a level of organization superior to that which existed previously to your reading this segment of the book.

One final time, as you are sitting there, take note of any present asymmetry. (Already, it may be less than it was just a minute or two ago.)

Now, consider the fact that you could pick up your left foot, your left leg crossing over your right leg, so that your left foot rests on the outside of your right foot. Then you could take your left foot back to its starting place and then cross your left leg behind your right leg, so that the front of your left ankle makes contact with the back of your right ankle. Then you could use your left leg to pick up your right leg. After that, you could return your left leg to its original position.

You could also interlace the fingers of your left hand with the fingers of your right hand in such a way that your left thumb is on top of your right thumb. Then you could separate your hands and interlace them once again, but this time with your right thumb on top of your left thumb. You could also, having separated your hands, place your left wrist on top of your right wrist, and you could place your right wrist on top of your left wrist, and you could repeat that movement any number of times. Finally, you could place your right hand on your left shoulder. Keeping it there, you could place your left hand on your right shoulder. Then you could bring your elbows up to shoulder height and bring them down again, keeping your right hand on your left shoulder, and your left hand on your right shoulder. You could do that several times, raising and lowering your arms with your hands on your shoulders, and then you could just allow your hands to rest as they normally would be.

Now, notice how you are sitting, and if you have become more symmetrical. Stand up and make the same observations, and then make them while walking. If you are now, as is probable, more symmetrical, do you feel that anything else is better than it was at the start of the exercise? Has the transference from one hemisphere of your brain through the other hemisphere of your brain effected a transference of learning, or has it just restored both sides of your body to the state that prevailed before one side was altered? The "work" that altered one side of your body took quite a long time to accomplish. **Notice how quickly and easily your brain has returned you to a state of symmetry.**

10

Exploring Altered States

*T*his NEUROSPEAK *exercise is somewhat different from the ones you have done up to now. In this case, what we seek to achieve is not the alteration of one or a few parts or functions, but rather a more generalized experience **extending throughout your body.** You should recognize, by the time we are finished, that you are exploring altered states of consciousness and also a level of muscular and other types of relaxation quite recognizably different from your condition at the present time.*

When you get to the end of this paragraph, walk around the room a few times and take note of your perceptions—how you experience your environment and whether you feel relaxed or not. Notice how you are moving and whatever else you are able to identify with respect to your present way of being as you just move around the room. After that, be seated as described before—the same kind of chair, the same arrangement of the feet, and so on. Alter your position as little as possible while you read the text. Remember the importance of focusing your consciousness and remember that since the text is addressing your brain directly, you need to read rather slowly and very carefully, allowing a brief pause between the sentences, so that your body *can assimilate what you are reading and organize itself accordingly. Expect that the **altered state, and the relaxation, you are going to experience** will be pleasurable for you. Now, make your observations; then return to your chair and simply read.*

There are many systems which seek to further personal development and actualize human potentials. Almost all of the more sophisticated ones utilize experiences of breathing which do not coincide with the experiences of breathing most people have apart from such training. For example, while breathing it is possible to have the *feeling* of directing the breath through the body and to any part of the body. You can have the feeling, for example, of breathing into your left foot or into your right hand, or you can have the feeling of breathing up into your brain space and then of exhaling down into your pelvis.

A person can be asked to breathe down into the left foot and then to breathe up through the left foot, to direct the breathing up and down, so that it passes in and out of the foot through the bottom and the top of the foot.

The breathing can be directed down through the upper body and through the length of the leg into the right foot. You can breathe in through the bottom of your right foot, letting the breath come up through the right leg, on up through the upper body to the chest, and then continue on up through your head, through your brain space and beyond.

The breathing can be directed to your left knee and then back up, and down to your right knee. Then, you can breathe up to your nose and down to your left knee, back up to the nose and down to the right knee, and continue to alternate directing the breathing to your left knee and your right knee.

Your breathing can simply move up and down through your upper body only, so that the breathing passes in and out through the top of your head at one end, and in and out between your legs at the other end—breathing in through the crotch so that the breathing passes up along your spine into your head, and then out of the top of your head and back down again.

The breathing can be done so that it feels as if it is done just between your navel and your throat, passing up and down, back and forth, just between your navel and your throat.

You can have the feeling of breathing in and out between your legs, and breathing up into your left shoulder and back down again. You can breathe back and forth between the shoulder and the space between the legs. You can breathe alternately in and out of the left shoulder, and in and out of the right shoulder, your breath passing through your body, and in and out between your legs, as you direct it to happen in that way.

The breathing can be kept in the lower part of your head, between your chin and your eyes. You can direct it in and out of your left ear, and in and out of your right ear, passing through your face to your nose and back again. The breathing can also be directed towards the forehead, breathing into the forehead and then having the feeling that the breath passes in and out through your forehead. You can do this and have the feeling that your breath projects, like a column of some very subtle matter out in front of your forehead, and then with your breath, you can draw it back in and then send it out again.

Some of the most powerful changes are likely to occur when you direct your breath up into your brain space. This can be done by directing your breathing through your two nostrils individually, so that you are directing one column of breath into your brain's left hemisphere and, simultaneously, the other column of breath into your brain's right hemisphere.

Or the experience can be of just one column of breath moving in and out of your brain space, so that the brain space pulses, or expands and contracts. With that kind of breathing, it is possible to feel that your brain space becomes considerably larger as your breathing continues.

If the breathing is deliberately directed up into the top of your brain and on up into the skull beyond your brain, then it is possible to feel that your brain space expands, but by elongating—becoming longer. Your breath can go out through the top of your head and then come back down through the top of your head, passing in and out in a column that goes higher and higher as your breathing continues.

And should you breathe up and in and out of your brain space, it can be done in such a way that you alternate expanding the length of your brain space and the circumference of your brain space. With that kind of breathing, a person can begin to get a sense of the actual physical presence of the brain and the brain space or, at least, to have a *feeling that the brain is being sensed*, especially as the breathing passes in and out through the sides and through the top of your head.

There is also an experience of breathing in through your feet and through your hands, so that the breath passes through the legs and through the arms, passes through the whole lower body and the whole upper body, passes through your throat and your head, *throughout your body's entirety.*

Now, when that breathing is done, the whole body can be felt to expand and contract with your breathing, your body pulsating with that whole body breathing, so that your body can be experienced in its totality and all at once by means of breathing in and out through the whole of it.

Just consider for a moment that whole body breathing, your body's entirety *experienced all at once, a unified, harmonious whole.* Pause for a moment and consider that possibility.

Now, when you have completed this paragraph, just sit quietly and take note of how you feel—your state of consciousness, whether you are relaxed, your relationship to your environment, and whatever else you may notice. Then get up and walk around making the same kinds of observations. Notice whether you stand as before or differently, whether you feel a definite state of relaxation, and in what ways your experience of your body, yourself, and your world, may differ from your experience before you read these few pages. After that, be seated and just read the concluding paragraph.

It is likely that you are still having an experience of states of consciousness definitely different from your norm. It is suggested that you just relax further and enjoy exploring and examining your present way of being, making comparisons with your more usual norms of consciousness.

Then, when you have really explored your experiences so that you can recall them vividly, get up and walk around rather briskly for a minute or two. You may discover that you begin moving into a state of increasing alertness and wakefulness. Examine that state, too, and then try to be aware of how it gradually merges with a condition that feels more like your normal state.

11

SELF-REGULATING BRAIN WAVES

As usual, be seated with both feet flat on the floor and parallel to each other at the customary distance. As always, read carefully and slowly, pausing for a second or two between sentences. It should go without saying that you should never interrupt one of these exercises to go to the bathroom, answer the telephone, or for any other reason. Such an interruption guarantees a partial or total failure of your effort.

*We are going to work towards changes that are somewhat different from any you have experienced up to now—somewhat similar to, but not at all the same as changes experienced in the exercise "Exploring Altered States." In this case, we will attempt to give you some measure of control over your production of two kinds of brain waves—namely, **alpha** and **delta** waves. If you do not already understand the effects of predominantly **alpha** or **delta** wave production, it will be explained to you later. Additionally, an exercise like this one is intended to exert the same kind of beneficial effect on the part focused on—in this case, your brain—as on any other part or functions of the body upon which the focus of consciousness is maintained for a sufficient amount of time.*

You are generally aware of where your brain is within your skull. You probably know that your brain has two hemispheres—a left hemisphere and a right hemisphere. Consciousness can be focused in the space where your brain's left hemisphere is, or it can be focused where your brain's right hemisphere is.

It is possible to direct your breathing so that you feel that you are breathing into your brain's left hemisphere. You could do this for a while and, as you do, you are likely to discover that your awareness of your left hemisphere is quite different from your awareness of the right side of your brain. You can also breathe into the right hemisphere of your brain for a while, doing so many times, and then the apparent sensations on the right side will probably resemble those you experienced when you breathed up into the left side of your brain.

Remember just to read and not to engage voluntarily in the movements described in the text. You will undoubtedly experience in yourself a tendency or impulse to engage in these movements, but again, do not perform the movements voluntarily. Now you can also breathe towards the back of your brain, and you can breathe towards the base of your brain in the back, or you can breathe towards the middle of your brain in the back, or you can breathe towards the top of your brain in the back. You can breathe towards the back of your brain in such a way that you feel that your skull elongates in the back. You then can breathe forward through your brain and into your forehead, and then back again. You can breathe to the back of your skull, and you can breathe to the front of your skull, so that your skull elongates in the front as well as in the back as you breathe back and forth, finding as you do so that you feel that your brain also elongates to the front and to the back.

Your feeling of breathing through your brain is very effective in helping you to maintain your focus on your brain. Moreover, as you maintain that focus, you really will have a feeling that you sense not only the surface of your brain but also the interior of your brain, as you direct your breath through it. When you breathe into the back of your brain and into the back of your skull, the longer you continue to do so, the more you will feel that your brain as well as your skull elongates in the back. At first, it may feel as if it is only your skull that elongates as you direct your breathing through your brain and into your skull. However, as that sensation becomes more vivid, your feeling that your brain is also being reshaped by your breathing becomes more clear. You can not only breathe up into the top of your head, past the top of your brain, creating a sense of elongation of your brain in your skull at the top of your head, but there are other interesting ways that you can create some novel sensations up there in your brain space.

You can, for example, breathe with your left nostril into your brain's left hemisphere, while simultaneously breathing through your right nostril up into your brain's right hemisphere. You can do this in such a way that you feel that your brain and your skull elongate out to the left on your left side and, at the same time, elongate out to the right on your right side. Then, when you exhale, your brain and your skull can move back in, so that you feel the two sides to be as they were before you inhaled into the left and the right sides of your brain. In other words, by doing this, you can create a sense of pulsations in your brain, your brain expanding out as you inhale, moving back in as you exhale, moving out as you inhale, and so on—gentle pulsations of your brain, pulsings experienced by you as very clear sensations of movements of your brain and of your skull.

Similarly, you can breathe up into both hemispheres of your brain, and beyond that up into your skull, again feeling that your skull elongates, but this time in upward *and* outward directions. That movement of your breathing up and down through your brain can bring your brain very clearly into focus again, can create again the feeling of pulsations.

After you have breathed into your brain for a while longer, breathing now backward and forward through your brain and then breathing up and down through your brain, you can *stop directing your breathing to your brain.* In fact, just forget about your breathing. Then you might find that, even without your directed breathing, your consciousness remains well focused on (or in) your brain and that you have what seems a quite clear sensory impression of the exterior of your brain, of your brain resting there within your skull, and perhaps even a sense of feeling below your brain's surface *into* your brain and a sense of some kind of physical activity going on in your brain.

Once your consciousness is focused on your brain's processes, feeling them or just trying to feel them, then an even stronger image of your brain may appear within your field of consciousness. Then, if you pause for a while and do *not* try to do or *experience* anything, it may be that you will have a sense of *your brain just quietly floating there* in your consciousness—an experience that some kinds of meditation practices have to work very hard to achieve.

Pause for at least ten seconds before going on to the next paragraph.

You can also have the experience of feeling that you are exploring your brain space with your eyes, directing your eye movements into your brain space. You can look up into your left hemisphere and let your eyes roam around it. Then you can look up into your right hemisphere and let your eyes explore that side. You can also explore the entirety of your brain space, circling with your eyes at different levels of your brain space.

Within that space, you can make diagonal circles, some circles slanting to the left, and some circles slanting to the right. You can make vertical circles with your eyes, and you can make horizontal circles with your eyes in your brain space. You can make fairly quick circles with your eyes in your brain space, and you can make slower and slower circles, circling at different levels in your brain space. You can circle very slowly in the middle, making the largest horizontal circles you have room for, and then you can let those circles become slower and slower until your eyes come to rest. Your eye movements *stop*. Then you may have the feeling that *your eyes are resting* somewhere *inside* your brain and that, except for your awareness of your eyes and your brain, your consciousness has *no other contents*—no thoughts, no images, just quiet and tranquility. *Just close your eyes and self-observe for a while.*

Now, you may or you may not know that your brain produces various kinds of electrical phenomena, including those easily measurable brain waves called *alpha, beta, delta* and *theta. Alpha* waves are the predominant waves of meditation. When the brain is producing mainly *alpha* waves, then there is a sense of relaxation and serenity. *Delta* waves, on the other hand, are the waves of sleep. When the brain begins to produce significant quantities of *delta* waves, then the person becomes drowsy and, if the *delta* activity continues, simply goes to sleep.

You may notice that there are some very characteristic eye movements which accompany your respective responses to the instructions that your brain will produce either *delta* waves, *waves of sleep*, or *alpha* waves, brain *waves of relaxation*. It may happen that as soon as there is any suggestion that your brain will produce *delta* waves, and even before any mention has been made of drowsiness, you will definitely feel your eyelids moving down as you move them when closing your eyes. That tendency to close your eyes is, of course, appropriate when you are producing brain waves associated with sleep.

On the other hand, the eye movements you are likely to experience when your brain is producing *alpha* waves, or when it is about to produce *alpha* waves, brain waves of meditation and deep relaxation, are movements appropriate to those states of consciousness, just as the tendency of your eyes to close is appropriate when your brain is in quest of drowsiness and sleep. With *alpha* waves, your eyes can be felt to relax. It is easy, with a little practice, to feel your eyes relaxing when you or someone else provides the instructions that your brain produce predominantly *alpha* waves. Or, at least, your brain is likely to accept readily such suggestions when your consciousness is focused on your brain or your brain space.

Suggestions about producing *delta* or *alpha* waves may not only yield experiences of your eyes tending to close or to relax but also *changes in your breathing*. You may note three different kinds of breathing—that which occurs when *delta* waves are suggested, that which occurs when *alpha* waves are suggested, and that which occurs when no suggestions about brain waves are made. I will not tell you *how* your breathing may change in each of those situations. Try to discover that for yourself. But keep in mind that if there are *spontaneous eye movement changes*, or *spontaneous changes in breathing*, or *both*, then it is almost certainly true that there have also been changes in the kinds of brain waves you are producing.

To repeat, *your* focus on *your* brain can enable *you* to gain some measure of control over *alpha, delta,* and other brain waves. Your brain becomes *increasingly responsive* to suggestions about what kinds of brain waves it is going to produce. Then, if the verbal suggestion is given that your brain produce *alpha* waves, a state of relaxation will be experienced. Then if you suggest that your brain begin to produce *delta* waves, a state of drowsiness may very quickly result. After that, you can use the suggestions to explore the relaxed *alpha* state for a while and then the drowsy *delta* state for a while, going back and forth between those two states. To maintain the capacity, other movements should not be made.

When you have completed this paragraph, talk to your brain and give it the suggestion that it produce **alpha** waves, and then simply observe the results. Having continued with that suggestion and those observations for a while, then suggest to your brain that it produce **delta** waves of drowsiness, and observe what happens. Move every now and then back and forth between those two states, and notice whether it seems to you that as a result of your reading, your brain is willing to produce particular kinds of waves according to your instructions, at least to some extent.

12

INTEGRATING THE WORLDS OF THE SENSES

*It is only in rather primitive people or people who have managed to remain close to nature that there still exists a naturally occurring balanced multisensory experience of the external world—that world which exists **outside** of a particular person. I am speaking of a way of experiencing the world that makes simultaneous and approximately equal use of the senses, so that those senses render the **available** world as it is and not just fragments of it.*

Even one or two centuries ago, it was common for people to have a multisensory awareness of external reality. Now, however, we humans have reached a point of such estrangement from nature and of such inner fragmentation and imbalance that it is almost impossible to find anyone who does not falsify his or her world by bringing to bear upon it only one or two senses at a time, thereby diluting and distorting the reality experienced. In other words, some parts of reality are overemphasized, some parts are underemphasized, and some parts are overlooked altogether.

Imagine a photograph of a landscape. Then erase certain parts of the landscape, darken other parts of it, make other parts pale, and observe whether it is still recognizable as the landscape depicted in the photograph originally. That is what happens to the external world when the senses are brought to bear upon it unevenly.

It is easy to demonstrate that hearing suffers when consciousness is focused visually. Or that vision suffers when the emphasis is on hearing. If you emphasize awareness of what you are touching, you will find that there is a diminished acuity of both seeing and hearing, along with whatever other sensations happen to be available. Close your eyes, and you will almost certainly find that you vivify whatever other sense you then focus on.

It does not matter what kind of sensory experience is under consideration. A focus on movement sensations will dilute all the others. So, too, will a focus on tasting or smelling. Again, it is almost impossible to find a man who can stand in a room or pass through a room and be aware equally of what there is to be seen and heard and touched and smelled, of his movements, or of what he is tasting, should he be tasting something. No, he will be aware primarily of one of his senses, secondarily of another, slightly more of a third, still more slightly of a fourth, and probably aware of no more than that—if he is aware of that much. So how can such a person hope to have an adequate experience of the objective world?

This inability to utilize the senses harmoniously and in concert is a fundamental source of error. There are, of course, many other distortions of reality as it is experienced by the average person. In many cases, there is an almost total inability to think and, simultaneously, to sense more than *what is absolutely necessary to keep from bumping into objects or from falling down. Emotions, of course, may obstruct both thinking and sensing. Preconceptions of many different kinds distort the individual's sensing of his or her world. With all of these factors present, the reality of the average person is little more than a vague and bizarre approximation of what he or she would perceive if able to utilize the sensory, intellectual, and other capacities a human being is equipped to use.*

Now, add to this a fact that is recognized by almost all the world's major spiritual disciplines—that the normal human being is "asleep," or awake in only the most minimal way, bearing a much closer resemblance to the notion of a somnambulist, or sleep-walker, than to the notion of someone in an alert, waking state. And, just as the somnambulist's movements are dictated by the contents of his or her dream, so the normal person's mental life is governed primarily by the involuntary images, ideas, and impulses which arise out of the unconscious mind to play themselves out in the arena of the pale and disfigured "reality" perceived through the confused and unbalanced haze of the senses.

Focus, if you will, on this book you are reading. What is it that you sense about the book primarily? Assuming that you are holding the book, you are probably touching a page or pages of the book and possibly also the binding of the book and its cover. As you hold the book, you may also be touching a table or desk on which the book is resting. Since you are reading, you also are looking at the book. In order to read it, you must have some awareness that the words you are reading have been typeset in black ink on a page that, apart from the ink, is more or less white.

You are touching the book, and you are looking at the book, and in order to read it you must also be moving so that your kinesthetic sense is also involved in this process. If you have any awareness of that, then you may know whether it is only your eyes that are moving across the page and down the page, or whether there is also some kind of side to side or up and down movement of your head resulting from movements in your neck as you turn your head and raise it and lower it, however slightly.

While it is not a part of your *reading* experience, there are almost certainly sounds of some sort which intrude into your awareness as you read. You might also be conscious of odors reaching you, and you might even be conscious of some kind of taste sensations in your mouth, or possibly you are just conscious of wetness in your mouth.

Of what are you conscious primarily? Are you more conscious of touching the book, or of looking at the book, or of the movements your body is making as you read the book? And what of your awareness of sound, smell, taste, and any other sensations such as wetness or dryness, heat or cold? If you were to construct a hierarchy of sensations, ranging from those sensations of which you are most conscious down to those sensations of which you are least conscious, in what order would you place them?

Do you know whether you were, in fact, aware of *all* these different sensations before they were brought to your attention? If not, do you know of which sensations you *were* conscious as you sat there reading before the different kinds of possible sensations were called to your attention? Could you, at a moment's notice and apart from any naming and enumeration, have constructed an adequate hierarchy?

Is it possible that your hierarchy shifted from one kind of dominant sensing to another as the different kinds of sensing were brought to your attention? For example, when you were reminded that you were touching different parts of the book, was it then the case that your tactile sense was dominant? Or *became* dominant?

When you were reading about the black ink on the white page, what was dominant then? Was it your visual sense? And had that been true before the appearance of the page was brought to your attention?

Similarly, what about your kinesthetic sense? Were you aware at all of any movement of your eyes or of your head before you read about those movements? There has been no mention of the larger hand and arm movements you need to make when turning the pages of the book. Had you been asked about your awareness of your kinesthetic sensing at about the time when you were turning a page, how would that have affected your hierarchy of sensing dominances?

At the end of the next two paragraphs, you will endeavor to reconstruct the hierarchy of sensations you experienced while you were reading those paragraphs. Before, you were not prepared for such a task of self-observing. Now, however, you know in advance what you are being asked to do. You are being asked to take note of your tactile experiences, your visual experiences, your kinesthetic experiences, your auditory experiences, your olfactory experiences, and your gustatory experiences, if any.

You know that you must try to be aware of whether you have those experiences, of the comparative vividness of those experiences, and of how, for example, your attempt to observe them affects your reading, your comprehension of what you are reading, and possibly also the organization of your body. For instance, as you endeavor to keep track of your basic sensory experiences, does that effort lead you to interrupt your breathing, tighten your shoulders, introduce tension into your neck, or otherwise make yourself more tense at the muscular level? Do you have any awareness, as you self-observe, of extraneous thinking or of emotions which are either a product of what you are doing, or are known to have, or seem to have some other cause? Now, if you have had trouble making those various observations, comparing them and constructing a hierarchy of them, then by all means read these paragraphs again and construct the hierarchy. If you need to, reread the paragraphs several times.

As already mentioned, it is exceedingly rare to find a contemporary person who does not use one or two senses at the expense of the other senses, so diluting parts of any given reality, and so creating a distorted whole. It is also the case that there are different types of personalities and personalities who tend to favor one sense, or perhaps two or three of the senses, at the expense of the others, and to do that almost without exception. Thus, one may use the visual sense to the detriment of the others.

Another may emphasize the tactile and kinesthetic senses, de-emphasizing comparatively the others. *Health* and *balance* require a more harmonious and better orchestrated *multi-sensing*. It is often desirable to focus selectively, but that sensory selectiveness should be a free choice, not something imposed altogether unconsciously.

Because this exercise is more complicated than the others you have done, you have been asked to make a good many more observations than you did in previous instances. You will be asked to make some others, now and then, as we continue. At the end of this paragraph, get up and simply walk around the room, trying to note as completely as possible whatever you take in with your senses. Also endeavor to note whether you are more aware of your movements, of what you are seeing, of what you are hearing, or perhaps, of some other kind of sensory awareness. Again make a hierarchy, grading your senses in terms of the intensity of your awareness as you moved around the room. Of what kind of sensing were you most aware, of what kind next most aware, and so on? Please do the walking and self-observing now, after which return to your chair, your book, and your reading.

As you read, it is called to your attention again that your reading and your experience here and now has several components—principally, visual, tactile, and kinesthetic, any others having only a marginal significance. Or such should be the case—although unwelcome noises in your environment might prove to loom larger.

Given what we have done up until now, you are almost certainly aware of the contact your hands and fingers are making with your book. You are almost certainly visually aware of the pages of the book, including the lightness of the page and the darkness of the print. Unless your awareness has ceased to benefit from what you have been reading, you should also be aware of movement sensations—not just of the larger hand and arm movements which occur as you turn pages or perhaps re-position your book, but also of eye movements and, possibly, head movements, or even upper back and shoulder movements. If your eyes move freely, it should not be necessary to move your head in order to read. However, if your eye movements are constricted, then you may have to move your head, your eyes riding around in your head like passengers. If your neck movements also are very inhibited, then you may even need to move other parts of your spine and upper body in order to read back and forth across a page.

In fact, it is rare that a person has much awareness of eye or head movements while reading. And, unless there is some discomfort, there may be almost no awareness of the parts of the body not immediately involved in the action of reading, as the eyes and the head and the hands and the arms are involved.

In the case of a truly healthy person, "healthy" including a reasonably complete body image and self-awareness, the person would know just as much about what all the other parts of her or his body were doing as about the eyes and head and hands and arms which were immediately involved. In your case, as you have been reading, it is unlikely that you had any sufficient awareness of what your feet and legs were doing, how your pelvis was organized, what you were doing with your shoulders, how you were breathing, whether your body was more or less symmetrical, and so on. Unless some part of you is in pain, your awareness probably included very little of yourself, except for your head and your hands and, even then, you probably had very little sense of what you were doing.

Do not confuse such insufficient self-awareness with "good concentration." Your awareness would almost certainly be no better if you were just sitting there doing nothing. Really good concentration coexists with a healthy self-awareness. You will comprehend more, not less, when you know what you are doing. That is true in part because, when you do not know, you are almost certainly using your body badly and creating some measure of discomfort which, while it may not enter consciousness, nonetheless is a distraction for your brain and nervous system.

This is not to say that there is no need to use one or two senses so completely that the use of your other senses is greatly minimized. The point is that the choice to do so should be within the field of your awareness and that the choice to emphasize the role of one or more senses should be appropriate to the situation or to your objectives. The person who fully commands his or her senses will have the ability to determine to what extent any particular sense is going to be used or not used. That would include what is sometimes called in psychology "negative hallucination"—that is, the ability *not* to see, or hear, or otherwise sense what is objectively there—to eliminate any sensory impression so that for practical purposes, it does not exist at all.

(That is the opposite of a "positive hallucination"—the sensing of something as if it were there when it actually is not there.) The person in complete command of his or her sensing can simply regulate sensory impressions as he or she is able to regulate the sound of a radio simply by turning the volume control knob up or down. Not many people have that kind of control of the sensory mechanisms, but the capacity for such control exists within any human being.

Your experience can, as mentioned, be very largely visual. It can be a visual experience of whatever part of the book you are reading. Or it can extend beyond the book you are reading to include the desk or table upon which your book is resting. And your visual awareness can keep on extending to include whatever may be presently within the range of your vision.

As you are reading, you can also find yourself simultaneously aware of visual impressions which are called forth by the words you are reading. Although your eyes may be looking just at the pages of your book, if you are reading about a herd of elephants, then you are likely to have, at the same time, some kind of picture of what a herd of elephants looks like. In fact, the picture you have of that herd of elephants will probably be of more interest to you than the pages of your book and therefore will be "seen" by you better than the book in some sense. The same will be true if you are reading about a sailing ship at sea, vast armies on the march, high mountain peaks, a waterfall, a couple making love. That kind of "visual" experience is also likely to occur if you think, for example, about your dog, or your cat, or some other much-loved pet. As your mind dwells upon that animal, your image of that pet will probably eclipse very largely your visual impressions of your environment.

It is also true that your focus upon some limited part of your environment will cause you to see what you focus upon in a very different way than you are seeing other parts of your environment which *could* be equally accessible to your vision. What occurs is not just that the vision is focused, but that there is an exclusion from awareness of what is readily accessible to vision. The choice not to see, or only barely to see parts of what the visual sense is perceiving may be the consequence of a conscious or unconscious choice. It is easy, at any moment, to look at a whole group of objects, observing each one with approximately equal acuity, and then just to focus on one of those objects and observe that the others fade into relative obscurity or even nonexistence.

Any one of the senses can be used in this way—always providing that the stimulus is not so intense as to take away the option of selective awareness. Under ordinary circumstances, for example, we will not ignore an object that is sharp enough to penetrate the flesh or hot enough to burn it. (That is not to say that we lack the potential to exclude even very extreme sensations—some people can so disassociate from pain that they can undergo surgical procedures without anesthesia and with very little discomfort.) Similarly, but within a lesser range on the continuum of our sensory potentials, we regularly sense, or fail to sense, the stimuli presented to us.

For example, you can move the sensitive palm of your hand up and down over a surface like the arm of your chair or over some other part of your chair or desk or table, and you can elect to create quite strong sensations in your hand by so doing. Alternatively, you can use your hand in what will appear to be the same way, but greatly diminish the sensations in your hand—either by largely ignoring them, or by touching something else with your other hand and attending mostly to that hand's sensations, or by focusing on one of your other senses, and so on. You can increase your hand's sensations by, for example, closing your eyes, and you could do the same by plugging your ears so that the sense of sound offers little or no competition to your sense of touch.

Your hands, as they hold the book you are reading, receive a number of different tactile sensations—from the pages of the book, from the edges of the cover of the book, from the jacket of the book, and so on. Those sensations, if you allow them to do so, can very largely fill your awareness. However, suppose you are reading about what it feels like to be immersed in very hot water, to run your fingers through the fur of some animal, to pick up something very cold like a large piece of ice, taking hold of it with both hands, or to have your body massaged with oil. Or you might be reading about trying to hold a squirming fish in your hands, or to examine with your hands the tusk of an elephant, or to feel the hot sand of a beach beneath your back while the sun warms the rest of your body. To what extent, as you read about these things, will you remain aware of your hands holding the book and the sensations you had when you were just thinking about the contact of your hands with the book? Surely there will have been some shift in your awareness as you are reading—just as your visual awareness shifted from the black print on the book's white pages when you were reading about armies marching and about mountain peaks and waterfalls.

As you are reading, your tactile and visual experiences, as it has just been demonstrated, are only partly determined by the book you hold and look at. Even more, they may be determined by the content of what you are reading and by the visual and tactile images called forth by what you are reading and, as you have probably observed, the *images* can rather easily occupy your consciousness more fully than your sensory impressions, at least under certain circumstances.

As you read, you are probably aware of at least some sounds in the room around you. Some minimal sounds will be made as you turn your book's pages and as, from time to time, you adjust the position of your book, picking it up and putting it down on the surface of your desk or table. However, most sounds of which you are aware are probably coming from some other source—a source inside of your room or a source outside of your room that is sufficiently powerful that the sounds are able to come into your room. Those sounds might be from inside the building where you are, or they might be coming from the outside—street noises, for example.

Again, it is the case that your book might provide you with *images of sound* which will occupy your consciousness to an even greater extent than do the other kinds of sounds just mentioned. Consider, for instance, that you might be reading about the sounds of different kinds of bells. You might be reading about small bells tinkling or you might be reading about large bells tolling in the distance. You might be asked to stop for a little while and consider the sound of the tolling of those bells.

You might be reading about the sounds of an opera, or a symphony, or the voice of a country music singer. You might be reading about sirens wailing, the clapping of thunder, the sound of a motorcycle, or of a saw cutting through a tree trunk. You might be reading about the sound of heavy rain falling on a sheet metal roof, or of the rustling of leaves as the wind blows.

It is likely that, as you read about these sounds, they will call forth auditory images that will compete with your awareness of any sounds about you, and also compete with any visual, or tactile, or other sensory awareness you had.

Now, it is quite possible not to have to choose between sensory stimuli and sensory images. There is no reason why you cannot walk along a beach with a keen awareness of the sun on your body and of the sand beneath your feet, the water up around your ankles, sensing clearly how you pick up your feet, bending your knees and swinging your arms as you listen to the sound of the water and also to the honking of horns and to a band that is marching down a street near the beach.

You can certainly be aware of how you are sitting in your chair, and that you are holding your book, and that you are looking at the pages of your book, and that there are sounds around you in the room.

You can know very well what it would be like to stick your hand in a bucket of warm water and to stir the water with your hand while sensing the movements in your arm, while you listened at the same time to music on your radio and, in the background, were also aware of other sounds coming from your television set. At the same time, there could be smells from your kitchen, and you could be chewing on a piece of steak or munching on a cracker. You could munch and smell and listen and stir and feel the heat all at once, more or less equally.

You can get up and walk around the room, and you can feel your feet touching the floor, and you can feel your legs moving, and you can look at the room around you, and you can listen to the sounds around you, so that at the same time, and without difficulty, you can be sensing your body's *movements*, you can be *listening* to the sounds in the room, you can be *looking* at what is in the room, and if there is something to *smell*, then you can also be aware of that. If you are eating, then you could also taste what it is you are eating, and you could do those things all at once and without difficulty. In fact, you might discover that you are seeing *more* than you saw when you walked around this same room a while ago. *At the same time*, you may very well be hearing *more*, while being *more* aware of your movements and *more* aware of the contact of your feet with the floor. You notice especially whether the objects in the room stand forth individually and with greater singularity than when you looked at them before. Probably then your perceptions tended to lump everything more or less together. Does seeing each thing in its particularity remind you of what you experienced as a child, when everything was relatively new and you were, therefore, much more aware of the different parts which together made up the whole of your world at any given moment?

Now get up and walk around and take note of what, in fact, you do observe. Which of your senses did you find to be heightened? Did you feel that you were more aware of **whatever** sensory stimuli were present? Did you find that you were sensing your movements more clearly and perhaps, in fact, that you moved more as you might imagine a primitive person or an animal might move—more lithely and with a greater simultaneous awareness both of your body and of its environment. Try walking around again now and observe carefully how your experience differs from your experience of walking around the room when you were asked to do it **before** reading to achieve a better integrated and more harmonious kind of sensory functioning.

13

NEUROSPEAK AND PSYCHOPHYSICAL METHOD

At this point in its development, NEUROSPEAK remains a frontier. Its potentials demand a great deal of further exploration. Among them I have mentioned the possibility of educating the organism to respond so well and with such refinement that words directed to the central nervous system could bring about changes in a great variety of body parts and *involuntary functions*. At this early and pioneering stage, my hope is that the range of NEUROSPEAK's effectiveness will extend significantly beyond anything that presently can be achieved by biofeedback or by hypnotic procedures.

NEUROSPEAK is so-called because it is a method of addressing the nervous system by means of the spoken (or written) word. If there is an advantage to using the written word, that advantage lies only in the fact that materials such as I have been presenting are more likely to reach a large number of people when offered in the pages of a book. It is also true that there is something dramatic—because so unusual—about using the printed page to make predictable and sometimes quite complicated changes in the human body. And, of course, no tape recorder, video recorder, or other equipment is required in the case of a book.

Apart from such advantages, however, the spoken word is definitely preferable to the written word as a means of eliciting NEUROSPEAK effects. The very act of reading interferes to some extent with that passivity of consciousness which allows NEUROSPEAK to work best. The reader has whole patterns of muscular activity developed over a period of years, which have become well established as *unconscious* habits. The careful observer can observe in almost any reader individualized ways of arranging the muscles and the skeleton, ways of breathing, of moving the head and eyes. While such behaviors may be largely or altogether unconscious, they definitely do involve making efforts which dilute and otherwise deform the consciousness which can be brought to bear upon the reading.

There is almost never any comparable and firmly entrenched habitual way of listening to such novel materials as are contained in NEUROSPEAK exercises. Thus, if one is listening, it is easier to give oneself over to the experience and, specifically, to follow the instructions about letting the message just "flow through" the mind and into the body. Also, and very importantly, the *timing* of the presentation can be controlled by the person leading the exercise—assuming that the leader has a much greater experience of what the timing ought to be, as well as of how to emphasize certain words and phrases in the text, and otherwise how to present it in order to facilitate the listener's concentration and quality of consciousness.

Despite the comparative disadvantages, it has seemed well worth doing to establish the fact that the written word can be used to bring about such predictable and complicated organizational changes in the body as can occur in response to the exercises you have just been reading and experiencing. We have demonstrated, at a *scientific* level, some facts about the mind-body interrelationship which have never before been presented in this way. When such a demonstration *can* be made, then it *must* be made! I have suggested that the future of *written*—as distinguished from spoken—NEUROSPEAK may lie more in the province of literature than of medicine and psychology. However that may be, anyone who has read this far should not need any further convincing as to the uniqueness of the experience.

As the effects of *written* NEUROSPEAK will be exceeded by the effects of *spoken* NEUROSPEAK, the effects of an identical or comparable exercise will be still greater if the movements are also consciously imaged—that is, imagined with an imagination which includes images of the appropriate kinesthetic and tactile sensations. Beyond that, the exercise will become still more effective—bringing about still greater changes—if it is done with actual, objective movements, and not just with subjective, imaged movements. In some instances, the greatest effects of all can be obtained by means of a blending of objective movements and subjective images within the context of appropriately *altered states of consciousness. There can indeed be no question of any system of exercise realizing its potential for changing human beings unless that system includes the organizing of consciousness into those states which are most favorable to reaching whatever goals are being attempted.*

NEUROSPEAK ends when what is demanded of a person is not just attending to language, but rather a considerably more active participation in the process—utilizing images, movements, states of consciousness, and including any combination of them. To make clear the differentiation between NEUROSPEAK and psychophysical work, the reader is asked to experience the following exercise.

You will remember that early in this book you did a NEUROSPEAK exercise titled "Movements of the Shoulder and Upper Back." Try to remember how you responded to that exercise. To what extent did the mobility of your right shoulder improve as compared to the movements of your left shoulder?

How was your body organized at the conclusion? Did you notice that the right side of your pelvis was lower, so that your body was tending to tilt to your right side? Did your eyes look right, was your head cocked to the right, did your whole body perhaps lean to the right? Did you find that your nervous system was experiencing a definite bias towards your right side, so that you sensed your right eye better than you sensed your left eye? Your right shoulder better than your left shoulder? The right side of your face better than the left side, your right foot better than your left foot—in fact, that you could sense the entire right side of your body better than you could sense your left side?

Try to remember what happened when you got out of your chair and walked around the room. Did your right arm and shoulder move better, and did your right foot make a better contact with the floor than your left one? And remember how it was when you made big circles first with your right arm and then with your left one, alternately bringing your hands and arms up towards the ceiling and then down towards the floor. Try to remember any other responses that you made.

Now, I am going to describe to you identical and very similar movements, only this time you should physically do the movements you are reading about.

At the end of this paragraph, get up and walk around and observe the movements in your shoulders as you walk. Compare the movements of your arms as you walk. Then stand and take note of how you sense your two shoulders—whether you sense them with about equal clarity, or whether one might be sensed with significantly more clarity. After that, make some big circles with your arms—taking your arms behind you, then overhead, then to the front and down, comparing the range and ease of movement in your two arms and shoulders. Make the circles moving your arms together, and then alternating the movements. Finally, return to your chair and compare your awareness of your right and left shoulders, your right and left feet, the right and left sides of your pelvis, the right and left sides of your face, and your right and left sides as a whole. Please get up and make those observations now.

Having returned to your chair, sit as you did when doing NEUROSPEAK. Let your feet be flat on the floor, parallel to each other, ten to twelve inches apart. Position the rest of your body as symmetrically as possible, and then try to retain that symmetrical position as you read on.

When you did this as a NEUROSPEAK exercise, you worked with your right shoulder. This time you will work with your left shoulder. First of all just note how clearly you are able to sense it—the top, the front, the outside of your shoulder, the back, and whatever else you can sense. Then take a moment to compare that sensing with what you sense about your right shoulder—remembering, so that you can compare again later.

Now, keeping your body upright, move your left shoulder forward and take it back again. Remember, this is no longer NEUROSPEAK, and you are physically doing the movements. Take your left shoulder forward again, bring it back, and do that a number of times before reading on. There should be very clear sensations occurring as you do those movements.

Now extend your left arm out in front of you. Reach forward as far as you can without bending forward with your upper body. You should find that this is a larger movement forward then you made just a moment ago. It is still, however, a matter of pushing and pulling from your left shoulder joint. Make at least ten movements like that, observing your sensations closely. Then put your left arm behind you, and take your shoulder back as far as it will go, return it to its starting position, and do that movement also at least ten times.

Now, let your left forearm rest on your chair arm (or, perhaps, on your left thigh), and push up from your left shoulder joint so that you bring your left shoulder closer to your left ear and also closer to the ceiling. When you bring your left shoulder down, let it go just as low as it will go. Try arranging yourself so that your left arm can hang at your side, and then bring your left shoulder as high as you can raise it, let it sink as far as you can lower it, and do a number of those movements. When you have finished, let your hand rest on your chair arm or on your leg, and notice whether your left shoulder now hangs somewhat lower than your right one. Also compare the clarity with which you sense your left shoulder and your right one.

Now, your left hand resting on the top of your thigh, make circular movements with your left shoulder. You can take your left shoulder up, and then forward, and then down, and then back. Continue circling like that with your left shoulder.

Make some small circles with your left shoulder and, when you have done a number of those, make larger circles with your left shoulder. Make a number of slow circles with your left shoulder, and then make faster ones. Try doing small slow circles with your left shoulder and then, after a while, make large quick circles with your left shoulder. Make circles of different sizes and at different rates of movement.

You should also reverse the direction in which your left shoulder is circling. You can circle backwards for a while, and then you can circle forward for a while, sensing as completely as possible what you are doing with your left shoulder and what those movements feel like.

Now put the palm of your left hand on top of the thigh of your left leg, just a little above your knee. Now, pushing and pulling from your left shoulder, take your left hand down your leg and then bring it back up your leg. Do not bend your elbow, but keep the movement in your left shoulder.

Now rest your left hand on top of your left shoulder with your upper arm at about shoulder height, and then make circles with your left arm, circling from your left shoulder. From that position, make different kinds of circles—clockwise and counterclockwise, slow and fast, large and small, all kinds of combinations as your left shoulder circles with your left hand resting on your shoulder.

Also with your left hand on your left shoulder, bring your elbow out in front of your body so that your left shoulder rotates in. Then put your left hand in your left armpit and bring your elbow forward. Now you will find you are making a different shoulder movement, so that the shoulder moves more towards the center of your body. Observe that same movement when you place your hand lower down on the left side of your body, and then keep placing your hand lower until the shoulder movement becomes quite restricted.

Something similar will happen if you place your left hand on your left shoulder and take your arm back behind you. Then your hand can move farther and farther down your body until, once again, you reach a point of diminishing returns, and there is almost no movement back by your shoulder, or in your left shoulder blade, or in the upper left side of your back.

Now, extend your left arm so that your left hand rests on the table in front of you, and make a light fist with your fingers. Then just roll the fist like a wheel to the inside, and sense the rolling inward of your left shoulder. When you have done that, then roll the fist towards the outside of your body, sensing that your left shoulder rotates out. Then just roll your fist from left to right, so that your left shoulder rotates in and out, and notice that the sensations in your left shoulder are very different than the other ones you have been experiencing.

Put your left hand on your chair arm or your thigh, and circle with your shoulder forward, and down, and back, and up—making very large quick circles. After you have done some of these, reverse the direction of your circling. Compare those circles—and your shoulder movements and sensations—with what you experienced earlier.

Stop. Just sit and notice now whether your left shoulder hangs lower than your right one. Notice also whether your pelvis has sunk lower on your left side, so that your whole body is tending to tilt left.

Take note of where your eyes are looking, and whether, perhaps, your head has cocked to the left, so that your spine is curving to the left, and that therefore your rib cage is bending in towards the center of your body on your left side, while it has lengthened on your right side.

Sense your body as a whole, comparing your left side with your right side. You will want to try sensing and comparing with your eyes closed as well as with your eyes opened. Observe whether your left side feels more alive, and especially compare the feelings in your left shoulder with feelings in your right shoulder. Try to feel that you can sense down into your left shoulder joint, as compared to the awareness that you have of your right shoulder.

Also, compare your sensing of your left eye with your right eye, the left side of your face with the right side, the left side of your lips with the right side. Circle as quickly as you can with both shoulders and notice the movements not only in your shoulders but in your left upper back as compared to your right upper back.

After reading this paragraph, get up and walk around, comparing your left side with your right side—first of all, how your shoulders and arms move, then whatever else you notice, such as the contact your left foot makes with the floor as compared with the contact made by your right foot. Then stop and make some large circles overhead with your left and right arms. Do simultaneous circles, and then do alternating circles. Make some circles by first taking your arms back, and some circles by first taking your arms forward. Then simply stand and compare your two shoulders and arms. After that, return to your chair and make any other observations you can make.

Finally, compare the difference between the effects of such psychophysical work with the effects of NEUROSPEAK. While both approaches lead to changes, there are differences. Psychophysical work is better suited to apply to those body parts and functions which are susceptible to voluntary controls. That is true even when exercising while seated in a chair and reading a book. NEUROSPEAK may have a much greater potential for reaching body parts and functions which are considered to be involuntary. NEUROSPEAK can be of great value when there is an inability to carry out functions which would ordinarily be voluntary.

Afterword

NEUROSPEAK is one of several main components of a larger system of neural and sensory re-education called PSYCHOPHYSICAL METHOD or MASTERS TECHNIQUE. The Method was developed as a program of The Foundation for Mind Research during the almost thirty years I have worked as Director of Research of that Foundation. The Method is part of a still larger inquiry aimed at defining and gaining productive access to latent or barely tapped human potentials. PSYCHOPHYSICAL METHOD mainly consists of the following:

1) MOVEMENT WORK: This includes several hundred exercises, encompassing a great variety of movements and many different kinesthetic and tactile sensations. There are also hundreds of combinations of movements, sensations, and images—both objective and subjective—used to program the brain to reorganize the musculoskeletal system and to improve and expand the body's ability to move and to sense with clarity.

2) IMAGE WORK: This component emphasizes the use of visual, tactile, kinesthetic, and other sensory images and an "image body" to bring about changes in movement capacities, sensing, and also mental and emotional

functioning. In other words, images are used to affect directly the physical body, or the sensory images are experienced in terms of an entirely imaged body, also eventually bringing about changes in the physical (body/mind).

3) NEUROSPEAK: The use of the spoken or written word alone to bring about various psychophysical changes. NEUROSPEAK, like the other components, can also be used in combination with the others.

4) ALTERED STATES OF CONSCIOUSNESS: The use of altered states to affect the outcome of MOVEMENT WORK, IMAGE WORK, or NEUROSPEAK. Those different components can be used to induce and deepen the altered states, or the altered states can be induced by other means. Particular states of consciousness are used to make most effective the application of the other components.

Those four elements together constitute the basics of the MASTERS TECHNIQUE or PSYCHOPHYSICAL METHOD. They thus differentiate it from any other existing system or method and provide a clear-cut organization that can be used easily and effectively for teaching purposes as well as for explaining what the Method is and how it works.

ONE-ON-ONE BODYWORK: The Method can be taught verbally to groups of almost any size, usually limited only by available space. It includes as well, however, a system of bodywork that is an extension, intensification, and amplification of the verbally directed work. It is particularly well-suited to both physical and mental health complaints of kinds which call for psychophysical re-education rather than for medical treatment. As the late Tom Hanna observed, in the case of problems typically brought to physicians, this includes about half of all of them. Eventually it will be generally recognized that some problems call for medical treatment and others do not benefit from contemporary medicine and require a PSYCHOPHYSICAL METHOD-type approach.

For those engaged in the practice of a spiritual discipline, PSYCHOPHYSICAL METHOD provides an extremely effective practice of mindfulness and concentration, as well as giving access to subtler dimensions of body and of being. This is specifically the approach that is taught to adherents of the Fifth Way, as described in the author's book, *The Goddess Sekhmet.*

The practice of NEUROSPEAK and of the other components of the PSYCHOPHYSICAL METHOD is greatly facilitated by working with the courses of audio-taped exercises and instruction available. Inquiries should be directed to the author at P.O. Box 3300, Pomona, New York 10970. Workshops in the Method are offered from time to time and have been conducted in many different countries of Europe and Asia as well as the United States. Two Training Programs have been held, and there are presently about seventy-five certified teachers of the work.

QUEST BOOKS
are published by
The Theosophical Society in America,
Wheaton, Illinois 60189-0270,
a branch of a world organization
dedicated to the promotion of the unity of
humanity and the encouragement of the study of
religion, philosophy, and science, to the end that
we may better understand ourselves and our place in
the universe. The Society stands for complete
freedom of individual search and belief.
In the Classics Series well-known
theosophical works are made
available in popular editions.